CONTENTS

MANET
PAINTER OF MODERN LIFE

Françoise Cachin

THAMES AND HUDSON

Was Manet the revolutionary artist, the inventor of pure painting? Was he the destroyer of academism, or the person who revived great painting – the Titian, the Velázquez or the Frans Hals of his epoch? Was he a great blunderer, or the one who advanced the course of the great painting tradition? Was Manet the one who broke all the rules to become the first 'modern', or was he, as Charles Baudelaire said, 'the first in the degeneration' of his art?

CHAPTER 1
SCHOOLBOY, SEAMAN, ART STUDENT

In a detail of a portrait Manet made of his parents in 1860 (opposite), his mother's hand lies in a basket of wool. All her life, Manet's mother encouraged her son's unorthodox career. Right: a red-chalk drawing by Andrea del Sarto.

An artist's childhood raises the question – genetically, as it were – 'Art is a circle. Through an accident of birth one is either inside or outside it,' Manet himself said, according to his friend Georges Jeanniot, implying that he found himself inside the magic circle of true artists by chance. In fact, Manet did not come from an artistic family environment, unlike most of the previous centuries' great painters. 'It's not a sudden shock to find that you're a bourgeois,' said Degas (bourgeois himself), when Manet defended a friend who had accepted a decoration. Manet was born into the middle class, and there he would remain. Still, he was destined to become the wisest kind of rebel: one who welcomes risks while preserving a fundamental regard for eternal values.

A birth near the Ecole des Beaux-Arts

Edouard Manet was born in Paris on 23 January 1832 at No. 5 Rue des Petits-Augustins (today's Rue Bonaparte), between the Ecole des Beaux-Arts and the Institut de France – the beginning and end of all successful careers in the arts. Manet, however, attended neither institution; indeed, all his life he would be regarded as their mortal enemy. A week after his birth, Manet was baptized at the Church of Saint-Germain-des-Prés.

His father was a highly placed official at the Ministry of Justice in Paris. As such, he belonged to the Parisian judicial bourgeoisie, with its strict moral standards, but he was also cultured and liberal-minded. A long tradition of opposition to monarchy or empire had bred republican conviction. His maternal grandfather Fournier had been a

Photographs of the young Manet (above) and his uncle (left), the jovial Captain Edouard Fournier, who, as a museum aficionado, played a major role in young Manet's vocation.

The entrance to Manet's birthplace at No. 5 Rue Bonaparte.

This portrait of Auguste and Eugénie Manet was painted by their son in 1860. Auguste was ill at the time and would die two years later. He would not experience the satisfaction of seeing this work accepted at the Salon of 1861 and had no inkling of the rejections that his son would face during the career that began so auspiciously.

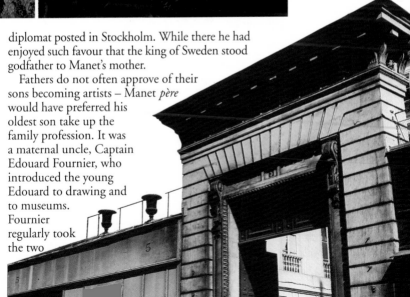

diplomat posted in Stockholm. While there he had enjoyed such favour that the king of Sweden stood godfather to Manet's mother.

Fathers do not often approve of their sons becoming artists – Manet *père* would have preferred his oldest son take up the family profession. It was a maternal uncle, Captain Edouard Fournier, who introduced the young Edouard to drawing and to museums. Fournier regularly took the two older of the three Manet brothers (Eugène and Gustave were born in 1833 and 1835) to the Louvre. Edouard's classmate Antonin Proust – future minister of culture and publisher, after Manet's death, of his valuable memoirs of his childhood friend – also accompanied them on their outings.

Proust remembers Manet as being an indifferent student at their grammar school, the Collège Rollin, as well as rather insolent. He recalls that once, during a history lesson, their teacher asked the students to read

Between 1844 and 1848, Manet attended the Collège Rollin (today the Lycée Jacques Decour), on the Avenue Trudaine (above). Though Manet had been born on the Left Bank, his childhood was spent across the river in the Batignolles section of Paris and in the neighbourhood of the Gare Saint-Lazare in the northwest, where he would later establish his studios.

For nearly ten years, Manet copied the masters, showing a clear predilection for Venetian painting. In 1854 he made this copy of Tintoretto's 1588 *Self-portrait* (left) at the Louvre, faithfully reproducing even the inscription at the top of the painting, which restoration work has since obliterated.

the pioneering essays of art criticism, *Les Salons,* written by the philosopher Diderot between 1759 and 1779. 'Concerning a reproach that Diderot had levelled against painters of his time for painting hats …that would soon be unfashionable: "That is extremely stupid," Manet exclaimed. "One has to be part of one's time, paint what one sees without worrying about fashion." ' Proust places this incident around 1846–8; Manet was then about fifteen, and was already interested in painting.

A precocious talent for drawing and caricature made Manet embellish his school notebooks with small sketches, and, seeing these, his uncle Fournier offered to pay for optional courses in drawing. Manet's pencil was from the outset an instrument of rebellion; according to his crony Proust, instead of 'copying the helmeted heads of models, he pencilled the heads of his fellow-students'. Did drawing and painting already embody for Manet his own form of opposition and liberation?

Copyists in the main gallery of the Louvre (above). The young woman on the tall stool appears to be making a miniature of the same self-portrait of Tintoretto. At the Louvre Manet made a number of the friends he would have all his life, among them Henri Fantin-Latour, Edgar Degas and Berthe Morisot.

*En rade de Rio-Janeiro: à bord du
Havre-et-Guadeloupe - ce 11 Mars 1849*

Manet the midshipman

Regretfully, Manet's father began to renounce the idea of
steering the unsuccessful student into a law career, but
was, for the time being, adamantly opposed to the idea
of his son becoming an artist. Did Manet himself, feeling
the need to escape, propose the idea of becoming
a sailor? However the situation came about,
Manet took the entrance examination to the
Ecole Navale in July 1848 – but failed. It was
decided that his apprenticeship had to follow
another route, and in December of the same
year, at sixteen years of age, Manet boarded the
Rio de Janeiro-bound training ship *Le Havre et
Guadeloupe* as an apprentice seaman. While
this venture did not turn him into a sailor,
these six months hardened the young Parisian
and exposed him to the realities of life at sea
and in the exotic ports of call he visited. In Rio
de Janeiro the young man was not unaware of
the Brazilian women, 'generally very pretty;
they have magnificent black eyes and similarly
dark hair'. And the black-skinned servant in his 1863
painting *Olympia* is perhaps reminiscent of a sight in Rio
that struck him deeply: 'I saw a slave market, it was a
revolting spectacle…the negresses are for the most part
naked to the waist…. Some of them wear turbans, others
arrange their hair set in tight curls very artistically, and
almost all of them wear skirts with enormous flounces.'

Manet fell in love with the sea, and he would vividly
recollect it in his superb seascapes in the 1860s. 'I learned
a lot during my voyage to Brazil. How many nights did I
spend gazing at the play of light and shadow in the ship's
wake! During the day, from the upper bridge, my eyes
never left the horizon line. That is how I learned the way
to put down a sky,' he is said to have told Charles Toché.

G uanabara Bay
(the Bay of Rio) as
the young Manet might
have seen it in 1849, after
fifty-six days spent aboard
the training ship *Le Havre
et Guadeloupe*.

F rom an 1849 letter:
'We were unable
to find a drawing master
in Rio; thus, our com-
mander urged me to give
lessons to my comrades
…it must be said that
during the crossing
I made myself such a
reputation that each of
the officers and teachers
asked me for a likeness,
and the commander even
asked for his as a gift. I
was delighted to fulfil all
requests, so that everyone
was pleased.'

Couture's studio

Back in Paris by June 1849, Manet again failed the entrance exam to the naval academy. This time his family at last consented to let him pursue an artistic career, his dream of so many years. Thus, in the autumn of 1849, Manet joined the studio of the historical and genre painter Thomas Couture, where he remained for six years and learned the business of painting. The choice of a master was well considered. Having some years earlier been a winner of the coveted Prix de Rome

Manet described his apprenticeship and the sailor's life in an exotic port in affectionate letters to his parents.

(recipients of which attend the Académie de France in Italy), at thirty-four, Couture was still a young fashionable painter, enjoying particular success with *Romains de la Décadence* at the Salon of 1847. Though a grand historical scene, the work was painted lightly and energetically and was not at all academic-seeming for the time – all aspects that no doubt attracted the young Manet.

The Couture studio was regarded as being among the most innovative. For learning painting, it was therefore a more daring choice, and was at first disapproved of by Manet's father, although in the end – showing himself to be more liberal than one might suppose – he respected the decisions of his seventeen-year-old son.

The years spent with Couture counted for a great deal more than modernist interpretations of his work – and Manet himself – would have one think. Couture's publication

Méthode et entretiens d'atelier (*Method and Discussions in the Studio*, 1867) shows what a fine and progressive teacher he was. Manet evidently drew and painted a lot during the course of these six years. The notable absence of canvases from this period – apart from a few copies – leads us to believe that Manet later destroyed this part of his work, produced under the influence of another artist and later repudiated.

Jacques-Emile Blanche, a young apprentice painter who came to Manet's studio at the end of his life to watch the master at work, was astonished by his knowledge of his craft. 'Manet was the last who knew how to use the methods and formulas that went back to the Spanish, the Flemish and the Dutch.' And, he added, Manet, 'probably the last to know how to handle the brush in a style that is in keeping with a magnificent

MÉTHODE

ET

NTRETIENS D'ATELIER

PAR

THOMAS COUTURE

tradition, appears to have destroyed even the tradition of the decadent – I mean academic – painters who saw themselves as the defenders of "French taste"'.

If Manet did rebel against his teacher, it was essentially against his objectives, the themes of his art. Couture was above all a history painter. For him, fine art consisted of narrative, allegory and respect for the past. 'On Mondays,' recalls Proust, 'the day when one set up the models' poses

Couture's large work *Romains de la Décadence* (1847, opposite above) was the artist's masterpiece. Today it is famous mainly for being an archetype of academic composition, created in an age of Courbet-style Realism. However, Couture's manner of painting and drawing was much freer than that of most other academic painters. Opposite below: a photograph of Couture and his signature.

Manet's drawing of a figure in Andrea del Sarto's *Baptism of Christ*, from the Scalzo cloister in Florence.

for the entire week, Manet had run-ins with [Couture's] professional models.... Climbing up on their stand, they would assume their customary exaggerated poses.... "Why can't you be more natural?" Manet would exclaim. [Couture:] "It is hard to be looked down on by a young man like you!... Thanks to me, more than one artist has learned enough to

set him on the road to Rome...." [Manet:] "We are not in Rome! And we do wish to go there. We are in

Paris. We intend to remain here." ' Another time, Manet had just succeeded in making a model adopt a simple pose and to keep some of her clothes on when, again according to Proust, Couture entered the studio. Seeing the clothed model, he made an angry gesture: 'Who was responsible for this stupidity?' 'It was me,' said Manet. Upon hearing this, Couture supposedly answered him, 'Come on, my poor boy, you will never be anything more than the Daumier of your time' (a mere cartoonist, a realist, someone low in the artistic pecking order).

Manet made many copies – both painted and engraved – of *Gathering of Thirteen Persons of Rank* (top), a painting erroneously believed to have been made by Velázquez. Also at the Louvre Manet copied (opposite) Titian's *Jupiter and Antiope.*

The museum as studio

Manet learned as much in the museums as he did in Couture's studio. First there was the Louvre, where he copied Italian works, including Tintoretto's *Self-portrait* (1588), two Titians – *The Virgin with Rabbit* and *Jupiter and Antiope* (1540) – François Boucher's *Diana at the Bath* (1742), Peter Paul Rubens' *Hélèna Fourment and her Children*, and an early 17th-century painting, *Gathering of Thirteen Persons of Rank*, which he presumed to have been made by Diego Velázquez (it is no longer attributed to him). Manet also made several visits to museums in Holland; his name

is listed on the July 1852 register of visitors to Amsterdam's Rijksmuseum.

The following year saw him making the traditional 'grand tour' through Italy with his younger brother Eugène. In Venice and Florence the two Manet boys acted as tour guides to Emile Ollivier, a future statesman in Louis-Napoléon's regime. In Florence Manet copied Titian's *Venus of Urbino*. From this painting he made his own irreverent version, *Olympia*, which he painted in 1863.

Emile Ollivier (top) was a young lawyer in 1853 when he met Eugène and Edouard Manet in Florence.

Living painters admired

He made a second trip
to Italy in 1857 and copied
Andrea del Sarto's frescoes
in the cloister of the SS.
Annunziata. According to Manet's biographer Edmond
Bazire, who came to know him only shortly before his
death – and who perhaps was able to glean information
from the painter's wife – Manet also visited Germany
and central Europe in 1853 on his way to Venice, seeing
museums in Kassel, Dresden, Prague, Vienna and
Munich, where he copied a portrait by Rembrandt.

Naturally, Manet admired a number of contemporary
painters. Gustave Courbet, for one, whose *Burial at
Ornans,* shown at the Salon of 1852 and reshown in 1855,
had sparked intense discussions in the studios. 'One
doesn't know how to say how good it is because it is
better than everything else,' said Manet, according to
Proust. 'But between ourselves, it isn't quite. It is too
dark.' He also liked the work of certain landscape
painters – a genre he himself did not develop until late in
life when he was forced to do so, 'imprisoned' as he was

Always copying the
masters! A draped
figure (above left) drawn
in red chalk after a figure
in Andrea del Sarto's *The
Arrival of the Kings*
(c. 1510) at the cloister
of SS. Annunziata.

This copy (above) of
Delacroix's 1822 *The
Barque of Dante*, made
around 1854 while the
painting was displayed in
Paris, is the only known
example of the fact that
Manet copied the work
of another
living artist.   *g. m*

in his garden by illness. Camille Corot, Charles-François Daubigny and Johan Barthold Jongkind were, in Manet's mind, 'the strongest of the landscape painters'.

Finally, there was Eugène Delacroix, whom Manet visited in 1855 to ask permission to copy *The Barque of Dante,* then on view at the Musée du

Luxembourg, the preeminent contemporary art museum of the period. The meeting was not a warm one; in fact, Delacroix fails to mention it at all in his journal. Even so, in 1859 the master gallantly rose to Manet's defence when he was being painfully confronted for the first time by members of the Salon jury, who would soon make him the most notorious of the Refusés.

The contemporary modern masters most admired by Manet's generation were Eugène Delacroix (photograph below) and Gustave Courbet, of whom Manet would make this lithograph (bottom of page) from a photograph after the painter's death.

● "There is a masterful canvas at the [Musée du] Luxembourg, *The Barque of Dante,*" [Manet exclaimed one day]. "If we went to see Delacroix, we could pretend we wanted to make a copy of it." "Take care," Murger told us, when Manet told him of our plan at lunch. "Delacroix is cold." In fact, Delacroix received us with perfect charm in his studio at Notre-Dame-de-Lorette, questioning us about our preferences and telling us of his.... When the door was shut behind us, Manet said to me: "It is not Delacroix who is cold; it is his doctrine that is passionless. Nevertheless, let's copy *The Barque.* It is quite a piece!" ●

Antonin Proust, 1897

❛ Re-creating historical figures,
what a joke! Only one thing is true:
to paint directly what you see.
When it works, it really works.
When it doesn't, you start again.
All the rest is humbug.❜

Manet (as reported by Antonin Proust)

CHAPTER 2
BAUDELAIRE AND SPAIN

Mme Lejosne gazes from beneath the large blue brim of her hat (opposite, detail from *Music in the Tuileries Gardens*, 1862). Manet met Baudelaire (visible just above Mme Lejosne, in profile) at her home. The bearded man behind Baudelaire is the painter Henri Fantin-Latour. Right: *The Exotic Flower*, an etching done in the Spanish manner by Manet, in a style reminiscent of Goya.

The confidence of the young art student from Couture's studio, his aplomb and his easy banter, made him an extremely popular figure, even before he had produced a single work of note. He and classmate Albert de Balleroy were soon ensconced in their own studio.

When Manet left Couture's atelier in 1856, already enveloped in this aura of a revolutionary – which earned him the admiration of the youth of his time – he was in no hurry to exhibit. 'Before taking on the Salons, I must call on the Old Masters,' he said. In fact, until 1859, Manet continued to make copies – of Tintoretto, Velázquez and Rubens – at the Louvre, where he met Henri Fantin-Latour and Edgar Degas, who were soon to become his closest painter friends.

Manet submitted his first work to the Salon of 1859, *The Absinthe Drinker*. It turned out to be his first rejection and his first scandal, but in a way also his first success. His budding talent was quickly defended by Delacroix, an important member of the jury, and by Baudelaire, a key figure in Parisian literary and artistic circles.

Apart from its deliberately sketchy technique, the relaxed drawing was calculated to displease the jury, since Manet's choice of subject was a drunk next to his bottle. The work was in no way allegorical, but in fact very real – the model was a known figure named Collardet – and was in itself a declaration of principle, and perhaps also a defence and illustration of Baudelaire's poems about wine, hashish and the sombre grandeur of the down-and-out bohemian character.

Even before his trip to Spain, the influence of Velázquez – who was known widely because of his engravings – on Manet is evident. Above: Velázquez's *Menippus* and *The Philosopher*, an engraving by Manet.

Opposite below: detail from an article about the 1859 Salon, with a preface by George Sand.

Baudelaire and Manet

Manet was well acquainted with Baudelaire. As a young man, he had probably met him at the home of Commandant Lejosne, a friend of the Manet family who played host to a wide variety of people, including the Manets, the critic Barbey d'Aurevilly, the illustrator Constantin Guys, the engraver Félix Bracquemond and the photographer Nadar. By 1859 the young painter and poet were already intimates.

ZACHARIE ASTRUC

LES 14 STATIONS DU SALON

AOUT 1859

PRÉFACE DE GEORGE SAND

Manet's *The Absinthe Drinker* (1858–9, above) was his first truly realistic work, and in making it he employed an aggressively sketchy technique, on both counts clearly breaking away from his classical training. Baudelaire's words were probably the inspiration for this image of the philosopher-drunk, a sort of Edgar Allan Poe of Parisian streets.

'We were seated at his home with Baudelaire, when the news of the refusal arrived; a discussion on Couture and Delacroix soon followed…: "The moral", said Baudelaire, "is that one must be oneself." "I always told you that, my dear Baudelaire," retorted Manet, "and was I not myself in *The Absinthe Drinker*?" Baudelaire just said, "Hm, hm." "Come on, Baudelaire is going to run me down! Why doesn't everyone have a go?.…" ' This discussion, recalled by Antonin Proust, shows us that Manet had a friendly supporter in Baudelaire, though one not completely without reservations. Baudelaire never wrote publicly in his defence, neither this year, 1859, nor in 1860 when the scandals of *Olympia* and *Le Déjeuner sur l'Herbe* were breaking. But one should remember that after 1859 Baudelaire published no reviews of any of the Salons, and each time the occasion arose he did support Manet in his own way. Perhaps the poet felt that Manet lacked the one thing that Baudelaire regarded as preeminent among the faculties: imagination. Or did he reproach his friend for what he considered to

The glass of absinthe in *The Absinthe Drinker*, an image suggestive of the drunken excesses of a Baudelairean 'ragman-poet'.

P. NADAR

205⅓1- Manet PARIS

Baudelaire and Manet photographed by their mutual friend Nadar. Baudelaire's death in 1863 – when Manet was only thirty-one – robbed the painter of an old friend and supporter. Had he lived, it would surely have been he, rather than Constantin Guys, who would have hailed him as the 'painter of modern life'.

be a serious character flaw: the pursuit of success?

But Manet knew very well that Baudelaire was fond of him and admired his qualities as a painter. 'There are flaws, shortcomings, a lack of assurance, but there is also an irresistible charm. I know all that, I am one of the first who understood it,' the poet wrote in 1865. Furthermore, he cited Manet in his last published piece of art criticism, on an exhibition of etchings in 1862: 'At the next Salon we will see several works imbued with a strong Spanish flavour, which would lead one to believe that Spanish virtuosity has fled to France. Messieurs Manet and [Alphonse] Legros are united in their decided preference for modern reality – which is already a good sign – this vivid and expansive imagination, sensitive, bold, without which, it must be said, even the best talents are only servants without a master.'

Fantin-Latour painted this *Homage to Delacroix* (1864, above). He presents himself in a white shirt, seated behind the elegant American painter Whistler, who, with Manet, frames Delacroix's portrait. To Manet's right are his friends Balleroy, Bracquemond and Baudelaire (seated).

Under the spell of Spain

Romantic literature – from Victor Hugo to Théophile Gautier – had made Spain fashionable in the late 19th century. One can also see, in the texts of Baudelaire, for instance, that Spain was being associated with Realism. For the young painter, the 'Spanish Golden Age' represented a model of reality and genre opposed to the classical models of antiquity and Italy so extolled by the Académie.

The whole philosophy of sublime rags, of the beggar-saint, in which Romanticism and Realism were happily blended, soon was to inspire Manet's *guitarreros*, pensive as poets (*The Spanish Singer*, 1860), his fancy-dressed children, charming and authentic as Sevillian *niños* (*Boy with Dog*, 1860–1) and gracious as princes (*Boy with a Sword*, 1861), and his dancers proud as duchesses (*Lola of Valencia*, 1862).

Surprisingly, before 1865, Manet had never been to Spain, and after his return he no longer painted 'Spanish subjects', apart from one bullfight scene, which he did from memory. But his ultimate hero would always be Velázquez. This he knew even before his trip, though he could only really study the master's works in all their splendour in Madrid, at the Museo del Prado.

'What captivated me most about Spain, what alone was worth the trip, was Velázquez. He is the painters' painter.... The sight of these masterpieces gave me great hope and confidence,' Manet wrote to his friend the art critic Zacharie Astruc in September 1865. The painter's

Lola of Valencia (1862, opposite, whole painting and details) and *The Spanish Singer* (1860, left) enchanted Baudelaire and Gautier.

predilection for the Spanish school earned him his first major success in May 1861. *The Spanish Singer* was admitted to the Salon, as was the *Portrait of M. and Mme Auguste Manet* (his parents), and he was rewarded with an honourable mention and a laudatory review by Gautier. For the first time, Manet's energetic technique and his sense of colour, set off by his use of black, were recognized. He himself said that in painting *The Spanish Singer*, he was thinking 'of the masters from

● *Caramba!* Here is a *guitarrero* who doesn't come from the Opéra Comique.... Velázquez would have greeted him with a little friendly wink, while Goya would have asked for a match to light his *papelito*.... There is a lot of talent in this figure with its unaffected grandeur, with its paint laid on in impasto, with a bold brush and in very authentic colour.●

Théophile Gautier

Madrid and also of [Frans] Hals'. Manet felt a strong association between the painter of Haarlem and Spain: 'I cannot get out of my head', he said, 'the idea that Frans Hals must have been of Spanish descent. There would be nothing surprising about that. He was from Mechelen' (a city occupied by Spain in the 16th century).

With this first success, a small admiring coterie formed around Manet. He must have thought – for an instant at least – that he had attained lasting glory, no doubt making it all the more difficult to bear his repeated failures at the Salon over the ensuing twenty years.

From the Café Tortoni to the Tuileries Gardens

For the moment, however, Manet was in fashion and led the life of a bohemian dandy. 'He went almost daily to the Tuileries from two o'clock to four o'clock, doing studies *en plein air,* under the trees, of children playing and groups of nursemaids relaxing on chairs. Baudelaire was his usual companion. People watched with curiosity as this fashionably dressed painter set up his canvas, took up brush and palette, and painted with as much composure as if he were in his own studio.' Proust's words, written at the end of the century with the aim of making Manet appear to be the father of Impressionism, lead one to believe that Manet executed his paintings outdoors. This was not the case, however; Manet did make small sketches outdoors, but he only painted in his studio.

On the Boulevard des Italiens, the terrace of the Café Tortoni, a popular gathering place among the elegant bohemians of mid-19th- century Paris.

'The Café Tortoni was the restaurant where he lunched before going to the Tuileries, and where, on his return between five to six o'clock, he would accept compliments on his sketches as they passed from hand to hand,' Proust recalled. 'But [those from] the Butte Montmartre and the other side of the water stood watch, and the old saying that one has more to fear from one's friends than one's enemies was to come true for him. He was wined and dined at the Café Guerbois and at the brasserie on the Rue Hautefeuille [Courbet's haunt], but he was also envied. "This young man mustn't pretend to be another Velázquez," said Courbet. The convention-bound [the academic painters] rubbed their hands with glee to see that division ruled among the intransigents.'

In reality, nothing was further removed from Courbet's universe than the elegant, worldly bohemia in which Manet naturally flourished. *Music in the Tuileries Gardens* (1862) showed this society in crinolines and top hats, under natural light. The work seems to have been at least partially inspired by Baudelaire, who, ever since the Salon of 1846, had been urging artists to paint 'the heroism of modern life' and 'the spectacle of urbane existence'. But Manet's elliptical technique, and his deliberate retention of a certain sketchy quality taken from life itself, failed to please; the critics reproached him for 'scorching the eye as fairground music assaults the ear', and for his 'mania of seeing things as patches'. Today it is easy to imagine what younger artists like Bazille, Monet and Renoir must have found in this work, which – even more than *Le Déjeuner sur l'Herbe* – was a catalyst for Impressionism.

This India-ink drawing of a nook in the Tuileries (opposite) was made by Manet on the spot in one of his notebooks. Another sketch in the same notebook shows the face of the opera composer Jacques Offenbach (above) and the curve of one of the garden's chairs.

In *Music in the Tuileries Gardens* (1862), Manet amused himself by gathering his friends around him. He himself can be seen in his elegant beard on the far left (1). Next, Zacharie Astruc (2), seated under a tree, and Baudelaire (3) chatting casually with Baron Isidore-Justin-Séverin Taylor (4), a passionate promoter of Spanish art in France. The women seated in the foreground are Madame Lejosne (5) and Madame Offenbach (6), whose mustachioed husband, Jacques (7) – soon to become renowned for his operas *La Belle Hélène* and *La Vie Parisienne* – is sitting under the tree on the right. Just in front of him is Eugène Manet (8), standing, slightly stooped. (This younger brother of Manet later married the painter Berthe Morisot.) The person to the right of Manet, on the extreme left of the painting, may be the critic Champfleury (9). The painting was probably inspired by Baudelaire, who wrote, 'For the consummate stroller, for the passionate observer, it is an immense pleasure to be among the crowd, to join the ebb and flow, the moving, the transitory and the boundless.'

3

4

Where nymphs are hidden and children disguised

If the Tuileries presented a spectacle of modern public life, several of Manet's works from 1859 to 1861 revealed his private – in a sense his hidden – life while masquerading as Spanish- and Flemish-inspired works. Such was the case with *The Surprised Nymph* (1859–61) – which in fact was originally a section of a much larger work entitled *The Finding of Moses.* Manet probably separated it either because he felt he had failed to master his first, very ambitious composition, or because the large

canvas was too much like the history paintings that he had hitherto scorned.

The model for the pharaoh's daughter, transformed into a bashful and voluptuous bather, was none other than the woman who had been Manet's companion for the previous six years, Suzanne Leenhoff, whom he had met in 1849 when she was giving piano lessons to his younger brothers. At the time, Manet was only seventeen years old, and she, two years older. In January 1852 Suzanne gave birth to a son, Léon-Edouard Leenhoff, and it is widely accepted that Manet was his father, even though the painter never officially acknowledged the fact, not even to his closest friends.

Suzanne, who posed completely nude for *The Surprised Nymph*, resembles an opulent fruit, a cross between Rembrandt's *Bathsheba* and Boucher's *Diana at the Bath,* figures from two paintings that had recently entered the Louvre's collections and which Manet had studied. In another painting, *The Catch,* Manet depicted his clandestine relationship with Suzanne, with himself as Rubens, Suzanne as the painter's wife and his son visible in the middle distance, fishing from the shore.

The *Surprised Nymph* (1859–61), was a tribute to other painted bathers, including Rembrandt's *Bathsheba* (1654, opposite centre) – which Manet had studied in the La Caze collection – and François Boucher's *Diana at the Bath* (1742, opposite below). Manet cut his much larger original work, *The Finding of Moses*, to focus the composition on the nude, for which his companion, Suzanne, posed.

Suzanne: beaming good humour

Manet married Suzanne a year after his father's death in October 1863, and, despite more than one lapse, he remained very close to her throughout their life together. Her good sense, her kindness, her gaiety and her talent as a musician

– an excellent pianist, Suzanne kept abreast of contemporary music, even playing Wagner at the hospice where Baudelaire lay dying – all of these qualities were an undeniable source of stability for Manet. His letters to Suzanne when they were separated during the 1870 siege of Paris are proof, as are several portraits he made of her

Mme Manet at the Piano, painted in 1867–8 by Manet in his mother's apartment, where he and his wife lived. Opposite: a photograph of Suzanne Manet.

– her peaceful face and demonstration of her gifts as a pianist in *Mme Manet at the Piano* (1867–8) or the maternal solicitude

apparent in her attentive listening in *Reading*. Without ever flattering her, he extolled the generous charms of her body – Berthe Morisot called her 'the fat Suzanne'.

The painter Giuseppe de Nittis, who knew Suzanne well, recalled that 'Madame Manet had something about her that was rather singular: a graceful kindness, a simplicity, a candour of mind – a serenity that nothing could alter. One felt, in her slightest words, the profound passion she had for her charming *enfant terrible* of a husband…. One day, he was following a pretty girl, slender and flirtatious. Suddenly, his wife caught up with him and said with a hearty laugh, "This time, I've caught you at it!" "That's funny," Manet responded. "I thought it was you." Now, Madame Manet, a placid Dutchwoman and a little on the hefty side, had nothing in common with a frail Parisian coquette. She recounted this anecdote herself with her beaming good humour.'

The Léon mystery

Manet's relationship with Léon was more mysterious. It may be understandable that, during the first ten years of his relationship with Suzanne, Manet would have wanted to keep his liaison with Suzanne and the presence of the child hidden from his family. But in view of the obvious affection between mother and daughter-in-law – the 'Manet women' – why did he continue to hide his paternity after his father's death, and indeed, until the end of his life? It is quite possible, of course, that a slight doubt about his paternity persisted.

'It would appear that his wife is very beautiful, very good and very artistic,' Baudelaire wrote when learning of the marriage. 'So many treasures in a single female, isn't it monstrous?' During the Prussians' siege of Paris in 1870, Manet sent Suzanne letters filled with tenderness.

In any event, Manet raised Léon – who called him 'godfather' – as his son.

Léon posed often for Manet during the 1860s. He was the youngster with carrot-coloured hair in a black velvet outfit, rather embarrassed by his weapon in *Boy with a Sword* (1861), the little startled love-child by Hals or Velázquez, who always believed himself to be his mother's young brother. Léon, who also figures as the boy in *Soap Bubbles* (1867), and, most prominently, as the enigmatic adolescent in the foreground of *The Luncheon* (1868), whose vacant, sulky expression left no hint of the true relationship between painter and model, except a sort of reciprocal perplexity.

The young Léon Leenhoff in a photograph and as a Spanish page in Manet's *Boy with a Sword* (1861).

The arrival of Victorine

The fashionable world, presented apparently realistically, though with coded references to his own private life, was not the only subject that Manet treated at the start of the extraordinarily productive 1860s. The other side of Baudelaire's stipulations on painting found in his

❝ It is said that Edouard Manet had some affinity with the Spanish masters, and it was never more apparent than in *Boy with a Sword*. **❞**

Emile Zola

L'Héroïsme de la Vie Moderne (*The Heroism of Modern Life*), where he speaks of the 'milieu of ephemeral existences floating through the labyrinths of a big city', Manet showed through a whole series of pictures of wanderers, displaced persons and clowns.

These works included *The Street Singer* and *The Old Musician*, painted the same year as *Music in the Tuileries Gardens*, and the series of musicians and Spanish dancers on tour in Paris – of whom Lola of Valencia, thanks to Manet's painting of the same name, has remained the most famous – as well as several drawings and engravings. *The Bear Trainer*, *The Clowns* and *The Gypsies* also demonstrated this search for new themes.

The Old Musician was Manet's most ambitious composition. Nearly 2.5 metres wide and 2 metres high, it is painted in a realistic style that thrust him into competition with not only Courbet and Velázquez, but even the brothers Le Nain of the early 17th century,

At the age of fifteen, Léon posed for *Soap Bubbles* (1867), a traditional allegory about the precariousness of life. Above is a sketch of the young man a year later, at about the time Manet made his most beautiful portrait of him, in the foreground of *The Luncheon*.

whose popularity the critic Champfleury (Jules Husson) had just revived among the avant-garde.

Less spectacular perhaps, though no less gripping, was the reproduction of an encounter Manet had while wandering through a section of Little Poland, near his studio: 'At the entrance to the Rue Guyot,' Proust recalls, 'a woman was coming out of a seedy nightclub one hand holding up her dress, in the other, a guitar. [Manet] went straight up to her and asked her to pose for him. She began to laugh. "I'll catch her again," Manet cried out, "and then if she still doesn't want to, I've got Victorine".'

Victorine Meurent – who, in fact, did ultimately pose for *The Street Singer* – had by this time become a fixture in Manet's life. She had

Close-ups of Victorine Meurent's luminous face and brilliant hair (below).

already posed for *Mlle V... in the Costume of an Espada* (1862) and for a portrait of a young redhead with a starkly lit face. The remarkable Victorine was to become Manet's mascot, his accomplice in the scandals ahead. The patience with which she posed, her relaxed charm and gaiety, her freedom in love, her independence and her lack of shame, contributed greatly to the uproar set off by two paintings that were soon to make Manet the hero of the day: *The Bath* (known later as *Le Déjeuner sur l'Herbe*) and, of course, *Olympia*.

In *The Old Musician* (1862, opposite right), Manet created a rather bizarre and anomalous grouping, associating it perhaps with certain figures he had already painted, such as *The Absinthe Drinker*, as well as with others at the Louvre. The little boy in white recalls Watteau's *Gilles* (c. 1719, opposite left). The central musician resembles a Hellenistic sculpture of the 3rd-century BC philosopher Chrysippus, which Manet had sketched at the Louvre (left). The little gypsy in the foreground was taken from *The Stolen Child*, a work by Schlesinger shown at the Salon of 1861. As for the old Jewish man on the painting's extreme right, he was a popular model whose address was later discovered in one of Manet's notebooks.

Victorine adopted many different roles for Manet's compositions. One of the most famous naked women in the history of painting is here (opposite) very much dressed, disguised as a poor street singer, eating cherries at the exit of the nightclub. In the elegant déshabillé of *Woman with a Parrot* (1866, left), she sniffs a small bouquet of violets with a pensive and becoming air. Courbet had shown at the Salon of the same year a superb reclining nude woman playing with a parrot, a work that might have been made in response to Manet's *Olympia*. It is not impossible that Manet then appropriated the woman-bird theme, but this time completely clothing the subject of his earlier scandalous work.

Ｈistory has endowed certain paintings with the status of inaugurating a new chapter in art. There is a before and an after. This is the case for Picasso's *Les Demoiselles d'Avignon* in the 20th century; and, in the second half of the 19th century, rightly or wrongly, the same role was fulfilled by *Le Déjeuner sur l'Herbe*.

CHAPTER 3

'IS THIS PAINTING?'

In the foreground of *The Bath* (1863, detail opposite), more famous now under the title *Le Déjeuner sur l'Herbe*, Manet painted a superb still life: a basket of fruit carelessly overturned on the model's garments. On the left is one of Manet's numerous pen-and-ink portraits of cats, animals for which Manet and Baudelaire shared a great fondness.

On 15 May 1863 the Salon des Refusés opened in an annex of the official Salon, which was held in the Palais de l'Industrie. Two nudes shown in the official Salon captivated the public and the critics: Paul Baudry's *The Pearl and the Wave* and Alexandre Cabanel's *The Birth of Venus,* which was immediately purchased by the Emperor Napoleon III. But in the Salon des Refusés the curious public could view those scandalous avant-garde works that had been rejected by the official Salon. As many as seven thousand people visited the exciting and diverting Salon des Refusés on opening day. 'The exhibition was separated from the other by a turnstile. One entered as if one were entering the "Chamber of Horrors" at Madame Tussaud's in London,' recalled Jean-Charles Cazin, one of the Refusés. It is hard to comprehend today that works by such artists as Whistler, Cézanne and Fantin-Latour – all of which have since become respected and beloved – could have at one time excited such mirth. And, of course, the young Manet.

Corrupt taste

It was Manet, in fact, who proved the hero of the day with his contribution – a sort of triptych, whose central panel, *The Bath* (later renamed *Le Déjeuner sur l'Herbe*), was flanked by *Young Man in the Costume of a Majo* and *Mlle V... in*

CATALOGUE

DES OUVRAGES
DE

PEINTURE, SCULPTURE, GRAVURE
LITHOGRAPHIE ET ARCHITECTURE

REFUSÉS PAR LE JURY DE 1863

Et exposés,
par décision de S. M. l'Empereur,

AU SALON ANNEXE
PALAIS DES CHAMPS-ÉLYSÉES

'MY SON! TAKE OFF YOUR HAT! LET US HONOUR UNHAPPY COURAGE.'

the Costume of an Espada. Most critics were shocked, not just by the subject matter, but also by the technique. 'Manet will have talent the day he learns drawing and perspective, and he will have taste the day he gives up choosing subjects solely for their ability to create a scandal,' noted the critic Ernest Chesneau.

'I do not see how you can make a chaste work of art out of two students wearing berets and overcoats sitting with a girl wearing

The 1863 Salon des Refusés gave rise to many caricatures, such as this one (left) by the satirist Cham.

Opposite: a detail of the cover of the small catalogue published for the 1863 Salon des Refusés.

One need only compare *Le Déjeuner sur l'Herbe* and *Olympia*, painted the same year, to Alexandre Cabanel's *The Birth of Venus* (left) – a great success at the official Salon of 1863 – to understand why it is that Manet's nudes were so shocking but those of the academic painters (even though they were more lascivious and, one might say, hypocritically sluttish) were not. Cabanel's Venus is idealized, but in keeping with the taste of the day, and she modestly hides her face. Cupids flying above her indicate that this is a goddess, not a woman of the 1800s. She is painted in a smooth and sugary manner – 'in exquisite taste', according to the same critic who found Manet's nudes so vulgar and his manner of painting so brutal.

only the shade of the trees. But even more serious is the intention behind it. M. Manet wants to become famous by shocking the bourgeoisie...his taste has been corrupted by love of the bizarre.' Jules-Antoine Castagnary added, '*The Bath, The Majo* and *The Espada* are good rough sketches. There is a certain life in the tone, a particular honesty in the brush stroke, both of which are far from average. But beyond that? Is this drawing? Is this painting? M. Manet thinks he is solid and powerful, he is only hard; what is especially odd is that he is weak as well as hard.' Even a critic as discerning as Théophile Thoré found *The Bath* to be 'in slightly risqué taste', though he also noted that 'in these spurned works there appears to be a new beginning for French art. He is baroque and wild, sometimes true and even profound'.

From *Le Déjeuner sur l'Herbe*...

The centrepiece of the triptych, positioned between two brilliant works of Spanish fantasy, was actually entirely classic in inspiration. Connoisseurs, artists in particular, could not have misssed that. In fact, its group of three figures had been copied from a composition of Raphael's, *The Judgment of Paris,* which had been popularized by a contemporary, the engraver Marcantonio Raimondi, and which represented two river-gods and a nymph. It was well known in the studios of Manet's day. The only difference introduced by Manet was that, leaving the woman naked, he had dressed the two men in contemporary garb, thereby making their companion a 'real' nude of today, a woman undressed, whose clothes could be seen brazenly strewn in the foreground among the remains of a picnic.

It must be said that Titian's *Concert Champêtre* (c. 1508, then erroneously attributed to Giorgione), one of the Louvre's most famous paintings, is identical in content to Manet's notorious work. It is simply that

Two works done in the 'Spanish manner' flanked *The Bath* at the Salon des Refusés in 1863. On the left was *The Young Man in the Costume of a Majo* (above), for which Manet's brother Gustave posed. Critics deplored the vividness with which the red blanket had been painted, remarking that in this work, as well as the one next to it, the head ought to be painted 'differently from the fabrics, with more intensity and profundity' (Thoré).

no one was shocked any longer by the sight of young musicians dressed in the clothes of Titian's time next to a nude woman. In truth, Manet – though no doubt fully aware of the provocativeness of the canvas that he himself called the *La Partie Carrée* (*The Party of Four*) – was simply playing the part of a modern Titian. The allusion was clear, and perhaps more than the naturalistic nudity of the model or the sketchy, even careless, style of the landscape – a deliberately offhand backdrop behind models who clearly had posed in the studio – the real scandal was this placid defiance of high art. Manet was, in fact, measuring himself not against those who were winning the Académie's prizes in his own time, not even against Courbet, whose work he had obviously consciously drawn upon in painting his nude and the still life in the foreground, but against the great Spanish and Italian masters of the 16th and 17th centuries.

...to Impressionism

Many people have wanted to detect *a posteriori* in this scene of a nude under the trees the first manifestation of Impressionism. Manet himself changed the title of the work for his private exhibition of 1867 only after Monet had entered the fray with his own 'déjeuner sur l'herbe' (*The Picnic*, 1865–6), only this time one that truly was painted out of doors, at Fontainebleau. Did Manet sense the extraordinary innovation in Monet's work and want to impress on others the fact that it was he who was the progenitor of this 'new painting' and that he intended it to remain that way? The more or less conscious strategy that Manet pursued throughout his entire career could lead us to think that.

Here, gazing at us when she should be looking at the bull, is Victorine Meurent, disguised as a bullfighter. This context only served to heighten the model's femininity. 'An unusual costume and an unusual occupation for a young person,' wrote a journalist for the French publication *Le Siècle*. 'I confess that I'd rather see her pursue more tender conquests and... if I had to choose between a companion who excelled at making jam and one who was good at killing bulls, I would pick the former!'

'My God! What indecency: a woman without the least covering between two clothed men!... The crowd... thought that the artist had intended to be indecent and disturbing in his arrangement of the subject when, in fact, he was only looking for lively contrasts and authentic masses.... What must be seen in this painting is not just a picnic but an entire landscape, with its strengths and its subtleties, its foreground so large and solid and its background so light and delicate; it is firm flesh modelled with great patches of light... this corner of nature rendered with such fitting simplicity.'

'You needed a nude woman, and you chose *Olympia* [overleaf], the first one who showed up; you needed light and brilliant areas, so you put in a bouquet; you needed dark areas, so you put in a negress and a cat. What does all of this mean? You don't know, nor do I. But I know that you have succeeded in making a work of art, the work of a great painter, in other words, to render energetically and in a unique language the truths of light and shade, the realities of objects and creatures.'

Emile Zola, 1867

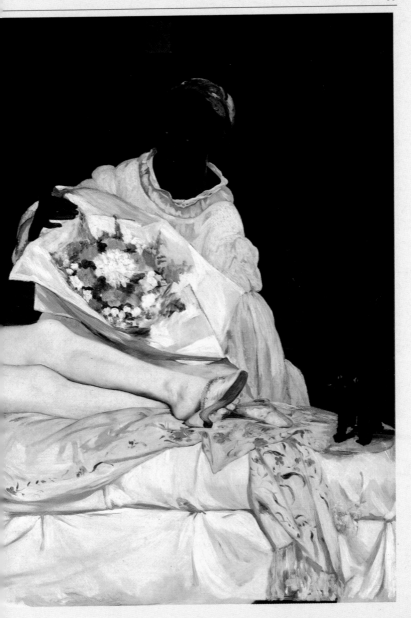

Olympia
La fille des Îles

But in reality, Manet's truly representative modern work, much more so than *Le Déjeuner sur l'Herbe*, was his *Olympia* – also painted in 1863, though not exhibited until two years later.

Victorine as Olympia

This odalisque (concubine), this harem creature (whose profession was unmistakable to the public at the time), was an agglomeration of Manet's most cherished paintings: a modern and ironic reincarnation of Titian's *Venus of Urbino*, which he had copied at the Louvre, Goya's *Nude Maja* and Ingres' *Odalisque*. In the juxtaposition of the two women, in this case one white and one black, the work perpetuates the long tradition of the odalisque and the slave, as did various works being exhibited at the Musée du Luxembourg at the time.

But Manet added to this altogether honourable genealogy the quiet impudence of Victorine, truly a 'free bohemian, a painter's model, a hedonist of the brasserie, a paramour for a day…with a cruel child's face and eyes of mystery' (the critic Gustave Geffroy).

> • *Olympia* shocked, aroused a sacred horror, imposed herself and triumphed. She was a scandal, an idol, a public presence and a powerful skeleton in society's cupboard. Her head is empty; a black velvet string isolates it from the essence of her being…. A bestial vestal virgin consecrated to the nude absolute, she bears dreams of all the primitive barbarism and animal ritual retained and hidden in the customs and practices of urban prostitution. •
> Paul Valéry, 1932

The copy that Manet had made of Titian's *Venus of Urbino* (left) was transposed in 1863 into *Olympia*. This 1853 photograph (below) toys with the fashionable eroticism of the contrast of white flesh and black flesh, so refined in Jean-Achille Bénouville's 1844 *Odalisque* (opposite left).

The black cat with its tail raised gave the work a note of erotic irony; with a sly wink to the art student, Manet substituted for the faithful dog sleeping at the chaste feet of the *Venus of Urbino* an animal that was believed to be satanic. Moreover, 'cat' in French slang is the word for the very thing Olympia is concealing with her hand. Perhaps Baudelaire had also inspired him: 'I should have wished to live with some young giantess / As at the feet of a queen, a voluptuous cat.'

Manet was by no means unaware of all that was embodied in his black cat. Indeed, X rays have revealed that the animal was painted in as an afterthought, most likely shortly before it was submitted to the Salon of 1865 – more than a year after the rest of the canvas was completed. This detail alone does much to show how ambivalent Manet was. On the one hand, he was completely devastated by the scandal his work provoked – a reaction confirmed by both friends and critics – and, on the other, he could not resist giving in to those irreverent impulses that would make things worse. Some of these impulses were better

For this nude study in red chalk, Victorine, the model for the *Olympia*, adopted a naturally modest pose. In stretching out her legs for the final position in the painting, modesty compelled her to cover her sex with her hand, a gesture which perhaps does more to accentuate it than to hide it.

hidden than others. Victorine's bracelet is an allusion to these lines by Baudelaire – 'My darling lay nude / For knowing well my heart / She had kept nothing on but her sonorous jewels' – but how many could possibly have known that it once belonged to Manet's very bourgeois mother?

Pantheism and the 'new painting'

A little black ribbon holding a pearl, and some mules, Olympia's only garb, have generated a lot of ink, including this from the poet Paul Valéry: 'Her head is empty; a black velvet string isolates it from the essence of her being' (1932). Michel Leiris used it for the title of one of his later works: *Le Ruban au cou d'Olympia* (*The Ribbon Around Olympia's Neck*, 1981). The bouquet reminds us that Manet was a dazzling painter of flowers – and would remain so until the end of his life – but it, too, proved shocking. A still-life, a 'secondary' genre, was here occupying the same plane as a nude, the nude being a noble genre when painted in an idealized manner 'after the ancients', but, in this case, mocked by the body's simplified naturalism. '[Manet's] real vice was a kind of pantheism, esteeming a head no more highly than a slipper, and sometimes assigning more importance to a bunch of flowers than to the face of a woman, as in his famous painting with *The Black Cat*,' wrote Thoré, in 1868.

This 'pantheism' was vindicated by the 'new painting', the new view of nature and art that – a few years hence – would be given the name that would make its fortune: Impressionism. It is significant that it was

Manet was always passionately interested in making prints, both engravings and lithographs. He was one of the founders of the Society of Etchers, an organization created in May 1862. That year his own engravings were acclaimed in the last piece of art criticism published by Baudelaire, 'Painters and Etchers', which predicted the revival of artists' original printmaking.

The Cat and the Flowers (1869, above) repeats a motif in *The Balcony*, which Manet was then in the middle of painting, but the little dog in the painting was replaced by a cat, Manet's favourite animal. This engraving was intended to illustrate a book entitled *Les Chats* by Champfleury, a strong supporter of Realism, for whom Manet had already created the famous poster of two tomcats on a roof, one black and one white.

Claude Monet himself, the incontestable leader of this movement, who, seven years after Manet's death, would organize a public subscription to buy *Olympia* and offer it to the State in 1890. The painting was exhibited first at the Musée du Luxembourg, and finally, seventeen years later, at the Louvre; there it was hung in the Salle des Etats, next to Ingres' *Grande Odalisque.* Thanks to *Olympia,* then, Manet triumphed – posthumously – even beyond his hopes.

'I painted what I saw'

Seven years after the *Olympia* scandal, a venomous article by Jules Claretie accusing Manet of once again 'firing off

● Like a man who has fallen in the snow, Manet has made an impression on public opinion.●
Champfleury to Baudelaire

● If the canvas of the *Olympia* was not slashed and destroyed, it is only because of the precautions that were taken by the administration.●
Antonin Proust

THIS WORK BY MANET WAS THE CULMINATION OF THE EXHIBITION. M. COURBET KEPT HIS DISTANCE FROM THE FAMOUS BLACK CAT. THE GREAT COLOURIST'S PREFERRED MOMENT WAS WHEN THIS WOMAN WAS ABOUT TO TAKE A BATH, WHICH STRUCK US AS BEING URGENTLY NEEDED.

a revolver' to draw attention to himself, provoked this response from the painter: 'What a silly thing to say!… I just paint what I see as simply as I can. Take *Olympia*, could anything be plainer? There are some harsh things, I've been told. They were there. I saw them. I painted what I saw.'

But by 1865, the catastrophic reception of his painting had nearly crushed him. 'I would like to have you here, my dear Baudelaire, the insults rain down on me like hail…. I should have wished to have your sound opinion of my work,' Manet wrote to his friend, who was then in Brussels. The answer was a famous letter that was plain-speaking but at the same time supportive and that clearly demonstrates the high regard the poet had for his friend: 'I see that I have to speak to you again about yourself. I show you your own worth. What you seem to expect is ridiculous. They make fun of you, their jokes upset you, they aren't being fair to you, etc., etc. Do you think you are the first man to find himself in such a position? Are you more of a genius than Chateaubriand and Wagner? They were both ridiculed. They didn't die of it. And, not to puff you up with too much pride, I will tell you that these men are models, each in his field, in a very richly endowed world, and you, you are but the first in the degeneration of your art. I hope that you won't resent me for the matter-of-fact way I treat you. You know the affection I have for you.'

The poet's usage of the word 'degeneration' probably did not do much to raise the spirits of the disheartened painter! But he knew Baudelaire well enough to understand what he meant, that in an era he condemned for its 'bourgeois and democratic stupidity', little inclined to elevate and recognize genius, his young friend not only was 'the first', but also represented hope for the future.

Olympia's black cat quickly became a symbol for the scandalous Manet. Théophile Gautier, who had defended Manet a few years earlier, found the work empty and dirty – in particular, the 'cat that leaves the trace of his muddy feet on the bed'.

Allusions to 'Michel's mother and her cat', a popular vulgar song, also turned out to be unavoidable. The cat, whose tail resembles a question mark, left the impression that Manet wanted to poke fun at the bourgeoisie. Left: a caricature by Bertall.

The role of shadow

The brilliant and charming Manet 'nursed neurasthenia underneath his breezy outward appearance', recalls the painter Pierre Prins, who knew him fairly well. A sense of drama and images of death are not uncommon in his work; they appear as early the 1860s, a full two decades before death cast its shadow upon him. He would then say to his old friend Antonin Proust that he 'always had the desire to…paint Christ on the cross. What a symbol! One could search until the end of time and never find anything comparable. Minerva, that is fine; Venus, that is all right. But the image of heroism, the image of love, could never equal the image of suffering. That is the root of humanity. That is its poetry.'

One should not underestimate Manet's religious works. At the same time that he submitted *Olympia* to the Salon, he had also sent *Jesus Mocked by the Soldiers* – the pair suggesting a sort of diptych composed of a degraded Venus and a Christ with a labourer's body (represented by the well-known studio model Janvier, who was also a locksmith), a double scandal to complement the publication of Ernest Renan's controversial *La Vie de Jésus* (*The Life of Jesus*, 1863), a positivist portrait of Jesus as 'a great man' rather than the Son of God. More than anything else, Manet's painting was about the drama of death and by no means merely another edifying 'historical tableau' of the sort he had produced the previous year.

The subject of another painting on this theme, *The Dead Christ with Angels,* submitted to the Salon of 1864, was a very naturalistic cadaver, a pretext for a brilliant 'piece of painting' – a proletarian body with the swarthy hands and feet of a worker placed like a still life on a white drapery and vaguely supported by blue-winged angels with pretty feminine faces who appear impervious to the tragedy before them.

To reproduce *The Dead Christ with Angels* as an engraving, Manet did a watercolour sketch in reverse.

Opposite: *The Dead Christ with Angels,* 1864.

Courbet made fun of Manet's painting, averring, ostensibly in defence of Realism, that he himself had never seen angels! Much later, Degas, taking issue with Courbet's jest, exclaimed, 'I don't give a damn about all that; there is a drawing in this *Christ with Angels*! And what transparency of paint! Ah! The devil!'

Yet another, *The Dead Man* (or *The Dead Toreador*), was cut from a larger work shown at the same Salon of 1864, *Episode from a Bullfight*, which was widely ridiculed. In a way this is fortunate, since it is only from caricatures that appeared alongside the scandalous reviews that the original work was able to be

‘I like the angels in the background, these children with their big blue wings who have such a sweet and elegant strangeness.’

Emile Zola, 1867

reconstituted. The bull was evidently microscopic, and the background comprised of the audience at the fight unconvincing, even in Manet's own estimation (his trip to Spain would not come

until the following year). In painting his dead toreador, he must have remembered more or less consciously the *Dead Soldier* (at the time erroneously attributed to Velázquez), a work he had seen as a child in the Louvre's Spanish wing.

We cannot know today what moved Manet, in 1877, to paint his very realistic-looking *Suicide,* though it

could have had to do with a tragic episode that had occurred over a decade earlier when he had discovered the body of one of his young models – the one in the *Child with Cherries* (1859) – hanging in his studio. (Baudelaire's *The Rope,* a tale dedicated to Manet, was also inspired by this tragic incident.)

About *Peonies in a Vase on a Stand* (1864), the poet André Fraigneau said, quite aptly, that it is 'the story of the death of a flower'.

A sort of morbid fascination was also present in a number of Manet's still lifes, dating – like *The Dead Man* and *The Dead Christ with Angels* – from 1864 and representing fish, or even flowers. These are meditations on death in the tradition of the *vanitas,* or macabre still lifes of the 17th century, though in Manet's style: somehow simultaneously lighthearted and pitiless.

In his 1867 show, Manet entitled this work *The Dead Man,* thus avoiding all association with folk-loric anecdote. Henri Matisse, upon discovering the painting in the United States in the 1930s, wrote enthusiastically, 'I saw it in the midst of a magnificent collection of works from all periods, between Rembrandts and Rubens, and it astonished me by the way it equalled its neighbours.'

Opposite above: an 1864 caricature of the original work, before Manet cut it up, retaining only the figure of the dead toreador.

Manet was a painter who in addition to his own genius had – like Delacroix before him and Picasso later on – the ability to attract brilliant writers. When Baudelaire, who had been the first to support him, died, the young thundering Emile Zola appeared to take his place. And when this staunch ally 'let him go', Stéphane Mallarmé materialized.

CHAPTER 4

PAINTER OF MODERN LIFE

All that one associates with Manet is in this painting, *Moonlight over Boulogne Harbour* (detail opposite and whole painting right), painted during the summer of 1868 or 1869. It is at once realistic – it depicts women awaiting the return of fishermen at night, observed from the window of Manet's hotel – and laden with historical references. Moreover, it is an admirable study in blacks.

When he defended Manet for the first time in the Paris newspaper *L'Evénement,* just after the jury of the Salon rejected *The Fifer* in 1866, Emile Zola was twenty-six years old. The following year he published a dazzling defence of Manet's work and of naturalism in general, which was at the same time a polemic on behalf of his own aesthetic beliefs. In Manet's work he had discerned a talent 'comprised of justice and simplicity'. 'I do not think it is possible to obtain a more powerful effect with less elaborate methods.... The place of M. Manet is decidedly at the Louvre,' he asserted, 'just as it is for Courbet, and for any artist with a strong and uncompromising temperament.'

Manet seen by Zola

Even if it eventually transpired that Zola misunderstood Manet's work and modern painting in general – notably

⁶ He does not retreat from the brusqueness of nature.... Since no one has said that, I will say it, I will shout it. I am so certain that Manet will be one of the masters of tomorrow that I believe that I would make a good deal, had I the means today to buy all of his canvases.⁹

Emile Zola, 1867

that of his childhood friend Paul Cézanne – and even if his vociferous defence of Manet, the man who best represented the avant-garde in 1866 and 1867, was deeply mixed up with his own professional strategies as a young writer, one cannot overlook the fact that he was the only one to put up a good fight on behalf of a painter who had none too many critics on his side. Armed with lengthy studio discussions with Manet, Zola knew how

Next to a photograph of Emile Zola (above left) is the title page spread of the novelist's 1867 pamphlet about Manet, with a portrait of the painter engraved by Félix Bracquemond.

• My favourite work is without a doubt *The Fifer* [1866, left], one of this year's rejects. On a luminous grey back-ground, the young musician stands forth, in uniform, red trousers with forage cap. He blows into his instrument, facing us. I said before that M. Manet's talent lies in exactness and simplicity, and I was thinking in particular of the impression this canvas had made upon me.... M. Manet is of a dry temperament, subsuming detail. He delineates his figures sharply...he goes from white to black without hesitation, rendering objects in all their vigour, detached from each other. His entire being compels him to see in patches, in simple elements charged with energy. One could say that he is satisfied with finding related values and then juxtaposing them on a canvas. In this way the canvas is then covered with a strong, solid painting. •

Emile Zola, from his first article on Manet in *L'Evénement*, 7 May 1866

to defend the 'new style of painting' with passion – and he did.

Manet's canvases embodied Zola's own definition of a worthy work of art, whether literary or visual – that is, 'a corner of nature seen through a temperament'. Zola was also the first of a long series of writers to grant Manet a 'formalist' vision, meaning that he was an artist for whom the subject was less important than the style and the manner of painting, though not, of course, ignoring 'nature'. No doubt Zola had in part taken up Manet's own comments: 'If you want to reconstitute reality, you have to take a few steps back. Then something strange occurs, each object assumes its proper place, the head of the *Olympia* is separated from the background in striking relief, the bouquet becomes a marvel of brilliance and freshness. The justice of the eye and the simplicity of touch have produced this miracle; the painter has proceeded as nature would have, by light masses, by large patches of light, so that his work has a bit of the rough and austere appearance of nature itself.'

Zola seen by Manet

The portrait that Manet made of Zola in 1868, which was accepted at that year's Salon, publicly announced the intellectual bond between the two men. Their alliance was indicated in the painting by means of several clues. Among the books Manet painted was the pamphlet that Zola had just devoted to him; the room is, in fact, Manet's studio, carefully rearranged to resemble a writer's study; the Japanese print, one from Manet's collection,

As in *The Collector of Prints* (1866, above), by his friend Degas, Manet portrayed his model in his *Portrait of Emile Zola* (1868, left) surrounded by objects – mainly Japanese, an indication of his modernist sensibility. Above Zola's pen – and the sky-blue pamphlet that he had just devoted to Manet – the photograph of the *Olympia* seems to be thanking the writer for his enthusiastic essay on this 'masterpiece which is truly the flesh and blood of the painter... the complete expression of his temperament; [which] embodies him entirely and which can embody only him'. Manet amused himself by changing the position of the head a little in order to direct Victorine's malicious gaze towards the future author of *Nana*.

suggests the passage in Zola's work in which he links '[a] simplified painting…to Japanese engravings, which resemble it in their strange elegance and their magnificent spots'; the small engraving after Velázquez's *Los Borrachos* must suggest conversations between Manet and Zola in

the studio about the Spanish painter; and the book Zola holds distractedly is a volume of Charles Blanc's *L'Histoire des peintres* (*The History of Painters*, fourteen volumes published between 1861 and 1878), one of Manet's wellsprings of reflection and inspiration.

Zola was not the only friend of whom Manet made a superb series of portraits. He painted Théodore Duret in the manner of Goya, doubtless remembering their visits together to the Prado (it was in a restaurant in Madrid in 1865 that Manet met the future critic and collector who would later devote his first serious work to the Impressionist painters); and Manet painted many portraits of his friend Zacharie Astruc – a writer, critic and sculptor. It is Astruc who nonchalantly plays the guitar in *The Music Lesson*.

The lady of *The Balcony*

In the late 1860s another face appears in Manet's work, one of a remarkable and unusual intensity – that of Berthe Morisot. This young woman painter, to whom

The person who was known within the artistic community as the 'handsome' Zacharie Astruc (left) was one of Manet's oldest friends. At the time of this portrait (1866), he was mostly a poet, writer and critic and had not yet become a sculptor. It is his rather mediocre poem that inspired the title of the *Olympia*. Astruc had been a defender of Manet in the press since 1863, three years before Zola. And it was he who planned the trip that Manet made to Spain in 1865. A man who, like Manet, was very enamoured of Japanese culture – indicated by the small volume on the table – he had probably introduced Manet to the art of Japanese prints. The very sketchily painted left hand was probably an allusion to Titian's *Man with the Glove* at the Louvre. When Fantin-Latour painted Manet among his friends in the *Studio at Batignolles* (1870), he showed him painting another portrait of Zacharie Astruc.

The three models in *The Luncheon* (1868, left) were as follows: in the foreground, Léon Leenhoff, as an adolescent; behind him was a family servant, and, seated in the rear, a neighbour and former member of Couture's studio, Auguste Rousselin. The composition remains enigmatic; the protagonists seem to ignore each other. Why are they wearing hats? Why did Manet borrow these arms, common props of more conventional painters? The black cat of the *Olympia* may also be found, cleaning itself, unaware of the strangeness of the scene.

Fantin-Latour had introduced Manet at the Louvre many years earlier, contributed her ardent and melancholy beauty to *The Balcony* (1868–9), an updated rendition of Goya's *Majas on a Balcony* (c. 1811).

The work was accepted at the Salon of 1869, together with *The Luncheon*. Once again, both works baffled the

critics: the first, because of the daring raw green of the balcony and the strange positions of the three figures; the other, because of the absurd assembly of objects with no apparent relation to each other – a lunch where

MORE STRANGE THAN UGLY' 73

oysters appear to have been served with coffee while a helmet and a pistol rest on a chair. 'Why these arms? Had the lunch followed or preceded the duel?' asked the wry Théophile Gautier.

In fact, both of the works were affectionate portraits of Manet's closest friends and relations, situated in settings that were suited to their personalities. In *The Luncheon* Léon Leenhoff is posed in the family's summer flat. As for the models of *The Balcony* – Berthe, the young musician Fanny Claus (taking off her gloves) and the painter Antoine Guillemet – these were three young artist friends of Manet, posing in a sort of Spanish parody, a comedy of elegant contemporary life.

Berthe Morisot – who in 1874 would become Manet's sister-in-law when she married his brother Eugène – was a very fine painter,

Berthe Morisot, photographed in 1873 (opposite below right), the main model of *The Balcony* (1868–9, overleaf), described in a letter to her sister her impressions of the Salon of 1869, where the work was shown along with *The Luncheon*: 'As always, [Manet's] paintings give the impression of a fruit that is wild, or a bit unripe. They are far from displeasing to me… I am more strange than ugly; it seems that the curious have been spreading the word that I am a femme fatale.' The landscape painter Antoine Guillemet and the violinist Fanny Claus, who played music with the pianist Suzanne Manet, were the other models for *The Balcony*.

one of Camille Corot's students who was later strongly influenced by Manet and Renoir and would become one of the most active and faithful members of the Impressionist group. Her charm and her intelligence, her talent as a painter and her wild beauty endeared her to Manet, and for many years she would remain one of his favourite portrait models. The fascination was mutual.

The protagonists of *The Balcony*, three of Manet's friends, appear to be playing different stock characters: the woman on the right is a sweet comic ninny; the self-satisfied dandy is in the centre; and Berthe Morisot, all mystery and drama, foreshadows the heroines of Henrik Ibsen and Anton Chekhov. Manet painted *The Bunch of Violets* (1872) posed on a fan in 1872, and then offered it to his model. Below: *Berthe Morisot with a Bunch of Violets* (1872).

'There's nothing greater in Manet's work than a certain portrait of Berthe Morisot, done in 1872.... Above all, it is the *Black*, the absolute black, the black of a mourning hat and the little hat's ribbons mingling with the chestnut locks...that affected me. The full power of these blacks, the cold simplicity of the background, the clear pink-and-white skin... the tangle of locks, ties, ribbon, encroaching against her face; this face with its big eyes, vaguely gazing in profound abstraction, and offering, as it were, *a presence of absence.*'
Paul Valéry
'Triomphe de Manet'
(exhibition catalogue)
1932

Contemporary scenes

In the 1860s, Manet revealed the broad range of his talent by painting scenes of contemporary life, though in a slightly contrived way, as in *Music in the Tuileries Gardens,* where he had 'made up' in the studio a series of figures under trees. Around 1867 – no doubt inspired by Degas, his friend and rival in modernism – Manet painted the astonishing *Races at Longchamp,* viewed not from an ordinary side view nor from before the start, but radically from the front, with the horses heading straight for the spectator.

During the course of two summer holidays spent in Boulogne, Manet painted several maritime scenes – mainly ones of ports – including *The Departure of the Folkestone Boat* (1869), a luminous, pre-Impressionist composition, and *Moonlight over Boulogne Harbour* (1868 or 1869), inspired by 17th-century Dutch paintings, which shows a group of women awaiting the return of the fishing boats in the evening. Manet loved to describe the various activities associated with the sea, whether they were of work – *Return of the Catch, The Pier at Boulogne, Caulking the Boat, Workers of the Sea* – or

Nadar, in his balloon, 'elevating photography to the level of art', was caricatured by Honoré Daumier (left). The same balloon appears in Manet's 1867 panorama of the World Fair (above).

leisure – *The Beach at Boulogne* or *On the Beach*, the latter showing his wife, Suzanne, and his brother Eugène all wrapped up against the wind.

It would be tempting to think that the funeral depicted in Manet's unfinished canvas *The Burial* (1867–70) is Baudelaire's (he was buried in September 1867), but we cannot be certain. The style is quite similar to that of a large urban landscape that Manet made that same year, showing the buildings of the World Fair. The scene was done on the spot and features strollers, members of the militia, dandies and a gardener, as well as a few familiar faces. One can discern the young Léon walking his dog in the foreground, and, at the top on the right, the balloon from which Manet's old friend and crony Nadar was photographing Paris and the fair.

Like Degas, Manet painted horse races during the 1860s. It was primarily the animation of the scene that intrigued him, probably more so than the horses themselves. Paintings or lithographs (below is the 1865–72 print of *The Races*), his works on the subject used a technique that carries one away.

Left: *Races at Longchamp* (1867?). One notices the extraordinary passion of Manet's stroke, almost as if he had been swept up in the race himself.

During the summer of 1869, Manet painted several scenes of daily life around Boulogne harbour: boats returning to port, sails slipping behind the wooden pier; the return of the day's catch by moonlight; and, as shown here, *The Departure of the Folkestone Boat*, a scene Manet could see from the window of his hotel room. (The boat whose twin smokestacks can be seen between the wheels is the one Manet had taken the previous summer for a short trip to London.) It is a beautiful summer day; the sea is high, and the sky bright; the women seek shelter under their parasols – the atmosphere and the style are already Impressionist. The woman in the white dress on the left is Suzanne Manet, accompanied by her felt-hatted son.

Manet spent the summer of 1873 at Berk-sur-Mer, painting seascapes outdoors. Oddly enough, these are less cheerful and Impressionistic than those he painted years earlier. In 1873 he seemed to be more interested in maritime labourers than in scenes of village or harbour life. Though a quintessential urban Parisian, Manet had a legitimately acquired knowledge of, and undying passion for, the life of seamen. In *Caulking the Boat* (1873), Manet shows fishermen tarring their vessel. The painter here returns to his beautiful effects of black and centred the painting around the contrast between the brilliant orange flame and the black tarred hull – recalling the contrast of the pink cape against the black suit in *The Dead Man* (see pp. 64–5). With Manet one is never far way from the 'pink and black jewel' evoked by Baudelaire apropos *Lola of Valencia*.

AUX AMIS
DE LA
VIEILLE GAÎTÉ FRANÇAISE

MUSÉE DROLATIQUE

THE TEMPLE OF TASTE

TIRED OF SEEING HIS WORKS REJECTED FROM OFFICIAL EXHIBITIONS AS A
RESULT OF SYSTEMATIC OPPOSITION, M. MANET HAS TAKEN IT UPON
HIMSELF TO ASK THE PUBLIC TO MAKE THE JURY'S DECISIONS; HE WANTS
JUDGES, WHOEVER THEY ARE, AND HE WILL FIND THEM.

> ❛ M. Manet has never
> wished to protest....
> M. Manet has always
> recognized talent where
> he found it, and he has
> not claimed either to
> undermine an old style
> of painting, or to create a
> new one. He has sought
> simply to be himself and
> not someone else.❜
>
> Manet, 1867

Below: *Portrait of Edouard Manet* by Henri Fantin-Latour, 1867.

The pavilion near the Pont d'Alma

The first of April 1867 was the
opening of the World Fair, in which
were displayed not only the latest
technological advances but also works
of art. Naturally the organizers
selected canvases by recognized
contemporary Académie painters
– Jean-Léon Gérôme, Jean-Louis-
Ernest Meissonier and Alexandre
Cabanel – but Realists such as
Camille Corot and Jean-François
Millet were given exhibition space
as well. Manet, however, was not
chosen. He decided, with Courbet,
to organize – at great expense – his
own private exhibition of fifty works,
to be held in a pavilion near the
exhibition grounds at the Pont
d'Alma. A letter to Manet from his
mother during this time shows her
very worried to see her son 'wasting'
his inheritance.

His finest works from the
previous ten years were all there

DOUARD MANET, – par G. RANDON.

LOLA OF VALENCIA

– an astonishing collection and the most complete one to date. There would never again be a retrospective of Manet's work that was quite so comprehensive. Unfortunately, there are no photographs of the installation. But there is an accurate log of sorts: all the works were caricatured in a pamphlet by Randon.

Despite a well-thought-out strategy – 'I am going to risk the lot, and, with the help of men like you, I plan to succeed,' he wrote to Zola – and despite the advertising in the exhibition catalogue, as well as the publication of six hundred copies of Zola's pamphlet on Manet, the exhibition met with neither critical nor popular success. Still, some people were very impressed, like the critic Champfleury: 'I was struck most of all by the way works conceived in various periods held up. From the first canvas to the last, there was total cohesiveness.'

THE PHILOSOPHER

Manet speaks

Manet himself wrote the preface to the exhibition catalogue, although he coyly discusses the painter in the third person. In it he defends himself as having been a victim of the jury and announces that he can no longer wait for an official endorsement: 'Since 1861, M. Manet has been exhibiting or trying to exhibit. This year he has decided to show the sum total of his works to the public…. The artist does

THE ARTIST

A few of Randon's cartoons of Manet's Alma Pavilion exhibition. They appeared in *Le Journal Amusant* in June 1867.

not say, "Come and see faultless work," but rather, "Come and see sincere work." ' In this preface one finds for the first time the word 'impression' linked in a positive way to the new painting methods: 'It is sincerity that gives these works a character that makes them resemble a protest, although the painter's only aim was to render an impression.' The term would soon be in vogue, but at first critics used it only derisively.

Although Manet's private exhibition was dismissed by

VISITORS' BOOK

the general public, it proved to have considerable and lasting impact on the pictorial avant-garde and would influence most young painters of the next generation, who were finally able to see Manet's oeuvre in its entirety – the majority of which had, of course, either been criticized or rejected for the past six years.

Manet was in a sense present at the Salon held that same year. Fantin-Latour had submitted a very fine portrait of his colleague, which was dedicated, 'To my friend Manet'. Every Salon visitor could thus see the

elegant and serious image of the painter who was so regularly the centre of scandal. 'Ah, yes!' wrote an anonymous critic, 'this very correct young man who is well groomed, well dressed, whom one would mistake for a hero of the turf, is the painter of the black cat, and who has been depicted as a long-haired dauber, with red hair and smoking death's-head pipes…. Now, if he had [earlier] been shown to have been so well turned out, the public might have been capable of granting him a lot of talent.'

Manet, painter of history

In the midst of the euphoria over the World Fair, news spread of the execution of Archduke Maximilian of Austria, whom Louis-Napoleon had installed in

'It's sheer Goya, and yet Manet was never more himself,' Renoir observed to the art dealer Ambroise Vollard in a discussion of *The Execution of Maximilian*. It is true that Manet's composition, even in its first rough version shown here (1867, above), was taken directly from Goya's *The Third of May, 1808* (above left), which he had seen in Madrid two years earlier.

In 1864 Louis-Napoleon had installed Maximilian, archduke of Austria (below), as emperor of Mexico without giving him adequate military support to resist the nationalist troops. Manet was in Boulogne on 1 July 1867 when a piece of shocking news began to spread through Paris: 'The Emperor Maximilian was shot on the orders of Juárez [Mexico's self-proclaimed president]. What a tragic dénouement to the ruinous and bloody madness of the war in Mexico!' noted dramatist Ludovic Halévy. Manet's work was obviously and justifiably felt to be the expression of his anti-imperialist opinions.

Mexico without giving him sufficient military support to defend himself. Overcome with indignation and perhaps identifying with the victim – he who was shot down symbolically every year by the Salon's jury and by the press – Manet, whose entire work had hitherto distinguished itself by its lack of historical referents, now decided to paint *The Execution of Maximilian*. For a year and a half he worked on several versions of the large canvas as well as on lithographs intended to popularize the work, since he would not even attempt to submit it to the Salon. The overall composition is similar to that of Goya's *The Third of May, 1808*. While Goya had depicted an event just before the execution – the soldiers taking aim – Manet chose to represent the most tragic moment – when the shots were actually fired.

There is nothing melodramatic about Manet's canvas. The scene appears to be frozen, the trio of victims dignified, and the soldier on the right, calmly reloading his gun, is the quintessential portrayal of indifference. In the final version, Manet dressed the firing squad in the uniforms of French soldiers, with the intention of stating as clearly as possible who he felt was responsible for the tragedy.

It may seem surprising that Manet – a confirmed republican who lived through the siege of Paris by German troops in 1870 and who, while not actually a participant, returned to the capital a few days after the bloody suppression of the Commune – would not have based another major work on the year's horrific events. But this time he limited himself to making a lithograph, *The Barricade,* a sort of inverted *Execution,* with a member of the Paris Commune taking Maximilian's place.

Barricade du F.S.t Antoine angle de la rue Charonne. 18 Mars 1871.

(1871, below) Manet
repeated in a Parisian
setting the composition
of the final version of *The
Execution of Maximilian*
(left). The victim had
been transformed into
a member of the Paris
Commune.

An event at sea

At the first Salon after the events of
1870–1 he showed a work produced
eight years earlier commemorating
the American Civil War. It showed
a confrontation off Cherbourg
between the Union Navy's *Kearsarge*
and the Confederates' *Alabama*.
Here, in what was above all else
a superb seascape, the viewer
participates in another sort of
execution, that of a ship in the
process of sinking after having been

hit by another vessel, just barely visible behind the first. Manet did not actually see this incident, though the fight had been announced in the press and large numbers of people had gone to watch it.

The following summer, in Boulogne, Manet again painted the *Kearsarge* in a series of seascapes, the only scenery he liked to paint – it reminded him of his early fascination for the sea as a sailor.

• M. Manet has thrown back his two vessels to the horizon. He had the knack of foreshortening them…but the sea that he swelled all around…is more terrifying than the combat.•

Barbey d'Aurevilly

COMBAT NAVAL
Par M. MANET.

Manet produced two more maritime paintings at the beginning of the 1880s. Both show an incident that had occurred six years earlier, when the polemical journalist Henry Rochefort had fled from New Caledonia – where he had been imprisoned in a French jail – to Australia in a whaleboat. The image of the escaped convict at sea evidently started to appeal to Manet when reports of Rochefort's amnesty and return to France began to circulate in the newspapers. 'I saw Manet; he was very taken [with the idea of creating] a sensational work for the Salon: the escape of Rochefort in a rowing boat in the open sea,' wrote Monet to Théodore Duret in early December 1880. (The turbulent 'open sea' in fact was re-created from memory in his studio.)

In these paintings, various aspects of Manet are portrayed: Monet's friend, trying to work in the Impressionist manner; the striving painter, adamant about forcing his way in to the Salon; and a bit of the history painter, though he took his inspiration from current events. Rochefort's boat seems so inconsequential in the middle of the sea; the event seems to have dissolved in the elements.

Even when it came to a seascape, the caricaturists could not forget Manet's black cat! *Battle of the Kearsarge and the Alabama* (1864, opposite) and the work as seen by Bertall.

In 1880, a government amnesty permitted the anti-imperialist polemicist Henri Rochefort to return to France. Manet then commemorated the journalist's escape from prison in New Caledonia six years earlier, faithfully following the narrative that Rochefort personally recounted to him.

' You understand, Manet is as important for us as Cimabue and Giotto were for the Italians of the Quattrocento. Because it is the Renaissance that is coming! '

Auguste Renoir to his son, Jean

CHAPTER 5

THE GODFATHER OF IMPRESSIONISM

*A*rgenteuil (1874, detail opposite), a painting shown at the first official Salon held after the Impressionists' debut exhibition, appeared to support their method of painting. This wash drawing of painter Eva Gonzalès's younger sister on the beach (1879–81, right) accompanied Mallarmé's translation of Edgar Allan Poe's poem *Annabel Lee.*

Manet opened up new directions in painting to many of
the young painters in France in the 1860s – including
Bazille, Cézanne, Monet and Renoir.
Collectively these dissenters from the
conservative guidelines of the Académie
were referred to as Realists,
Intransigents, Naturalists, or, simply,
'Manet's gang'. When they showed as
a group in 1874, they called themselves
Independents, but the name that
has stuck with them over the decades
is Impressionists.

The Batignolles studio

At one time they were also known as
the 'Batignolles group', after the part of
Paris where Manet had his
studio and where there was
an abundance of cafés where
the young people liked to
congregate: the Guerbois, the
Nouvelle-Athènes, the Café de
Bade. In showing his painting
Studio at Batignolles at the
Salon of 1870, Fantin-Latour
officially acknowledged Manet
– portrayed busily at work
in the centre of the canvas –
as the group's leader. Bazille
painted the same protagonists
in his own studio, also
granting Manet a central role,
in front of his easel.

John Rewald, the foremost
historian of Impressionism,
has remarked that 'Corot
attracted the timid minds of
the new generation, while the
more daring ones turned
towards Courbet and Manet'.
Even so, Manet could not be
said to have headed a school.

This is Manet's very lifelike rendering of a common Parisian café scene of the 1860s and 1870s (1869, left). Perhaps it is one of those in the Batignolles where Manet often went at the end of the day?

This caricature by Cham (1868, opposite) shows to what extent a young painter who refused to conform to the tastes of the Salon jury would be immediately associated with the chief scandal-maker Manet. The title is *Jury de peinture*, and the painters are asked: 'Do you admit committing this picture? Do you have accomplices? Are you part of M. Manet's gang?'

As Armand Silvestre recalls, he did not have the temperament for it: 'I never knew anyone whose

personality was more devoid of solemnity.' Nonetheless, he attracted these 'young Turks', as much by his charm and convivial spirit as by his talent and scandalous reputation. Though always exceedingly generous to his young friends – in his later years, he would financially support the more impoverished ones, especially Monet – he was still surprised and perhaps sorry to see himself allied with, even standing out among, those opposed to the Académie. At the Salon of 1865, in the middle of the scandal over the *Olympia,* Manet, to his annoyance, found himself being both congratulated and criticized for his seascapes! In fact, they were Monet's.

Manet welcomed young artists who came to see him paint or listen to him speak. On the left, one of them, Léon Lhermitte, has drawn him at his easel. On the facing page is a detail of Bazille's painting *The Studio on the Rue Condamine*, which commemorated a visit from Manet. From left to right we see either Astruc or Monet, Manet in front of a painting and the tall Bazille himself, observing and listening to him.

Manet and Monet

In fact, the men quickly became good friends. Cézanne also had a grudging admiration for Manet and loved to shock the dandy with his exaggeratedly bohemian manners, and Manet is known to have responded with affection to the admiration of Renoir and Bazille, but it is clear that he had most in common with Monet. Manet portrays him in works filled with fond allusions to the specific talents of the future master of

Impressionism. Monet is shown painting on his boat in the middle of the water – water being a major element in Monet's work both at the time and well into the future; he was also portrayed with his family in his garden at Argenteuil. For this occasion, Manet set up his easel outdoors – the first time he had ever done so – as if to pay homage to his younger colleague.

Manet competed against the man he called the 'Raphael of the water' on his own ground when he painted *The Grand Canal in Venice* (1875) and above all with *Argenteuil* (1874), a brilliant demonstration of this curious new technique called Impressionism. This canvas, partially completed out of doors, was shown

– IT'S MANET AND MANETTE.
– BUT WHAT ARE THEY DOING?
– THEY ARE BOATING, FROM WHAT I SEE.
– BUT THIS BLUE WALL?
– THAT'S THE SEINE.
– ARE YOU SURE?
– LADY, THAT'S WHAT THEY TOLD ME!

at the Salon of 1875, the one just following the first independent exhibition held by his friends. *Argenteuil* emerged there as a sort of manifesto in their favour; its naturalism was in keeping with their style. But it could also be seen as a challenge to this new form of modernity: the outdoor scene is primarily a double portrait of a pair of working-class boaters; it is more of a naturalistic illustration à la Maupassant than an Impressionist vision of the banks of the Seine.

Paris/Manet; Paris/Monet

The main difference between Manet and Monet became flagrantly apparent in two works they painted on the same day – 30 June 1878, to be exact – when hundreds of flags were unfurled in the streets of Paris in honour of the World Fair. Monet's *Rue Montorgueil* – a lyrical ode to the

These three works by Manet – all executed in 1874 – attest to his friendship with Monet during the golden age of Impressionism: *Monet Painting in his Floating Studio* (opposite above); *Argenteuil* (opposite below), framed by the dialogue and figures from a cartoon that appeared in an 1875 issue of *Le Journal Amusant*; and *Boating* (above), which portrays Manet's brother-in-law Rodolphe Leenhoff. This painting was felt to be disturbing because of the intense blue of the water and the lack of a horizon line (a feature reminiscent of Japanese prints).

flamboyant colours of the flags waving in the wind – contrasts with Manet's view from his studio, *The Rue Mosnier with Flags,* which is more austere and stranger. The banners are less important than the contrast of light and shadow on this Paris street, and the image of loneliness evoked by the man on crutches seen from behind and the halted black carriage cast a damper on the euphoric mood of the official celebration.

Paris was festooned with brilliantly coloured flags on 30 June 1878, in honour of the World Fair. Monet and Manet each produced a work on this theme. The canvases illustrate striking differences in their vision. Monet's *Rue Montorgueil* (above left) is as joyous, buzzing and airy as Manet's *The Rue Mosnier with Flags* (above) is deserted and melancholy. Left: *Man on Crutches,* 1878.

The next year, fascinated as always by urban projects, Manet was hoping to receive a commission to decorate the newly rebuilt Hôtel de Ville. He was interested in painting 'a series of compositions representing, to use an expression now hackneyed but suited to my meaning, "the belly of Paris", with the several bodies politic moving in their elements; that is, the public and commercial life of our day. I would have Paris Markets, Paris Railroads, Paris Bridges, Paris Underground, Paris Racetracks and Paris Gardens'. This ambitious project was never realized, alas – there was no response to his proposal (and perhaps, to be realistic, it would never have been feasible, since Manet's illness had already set in). Despite all his support for the new art concepts so brilliantly represented by the young Monet, it is evident

2ᵉ année.—Nº 29.　　　　**10 Centimes**　　　　Jeudi 16 juin

ALFRED LE PETIT　　　LES　　　FÉLICIEN CHAMPSAUR

CONTEMPORAINS

JOURNAL HEBDOMADAIRE

ADMINISTRATEUR : M. DUFFIEUX, 15, FAUBOURG MONTMARTRE, PARIS. — UN AN : **6 FR.**

EDOUARD MANET

that it was not places in themselves that interested him but the people moving about in them, and similarly effects of light only insofar as they helped to bring them to life.

A decisive role

'When I used to go see Manet on Sundays [at his studio on the Rue Saint-Pétersbourg],' recalls Proust, '[he] did nothing but praise all the devotees of the Batignolles school. He would set out all their works in the best possible light, worrying about finding them buyers, and forgetting about his own works…. He was taken with Claude Monet more than anyone else.'

Supportive as he was of them, Manet never participated in the Impressionists' exhibitions, except peripherally in 1876, when he loaned them Renoir's portrait of Bazille. This was not for lack of invitations. The members of the Batignolles group (less Bazille, who was killed in 1870 during the war) and Berthe Morisot all would have been glad of his presence. But Manet had excused himself from their first exhibition in 1874 and every time thereafter – paradoxically preferring to remain faithful to the Salon where he was so regularly rejected.

The quasi-official success he had in 1873 with *The Good Glass of Beer* made him even more determined than ever. This portrait – a rather banal composition painted in a Halsian manner in sombre tones – did indeed give the impression that Manet had finally fallen into line.

On the first page of *Les Contemporains*, this caricature shows Manet as king of the Impressionists, carried on his palette and seated on a beer barrel, an allusion to his work *The Good Glass of Beer* (1873, opposite).

He is an epicurean of the tavern – fat, red and jovial – and he believes in nothing so much as his pipe and his beer, said one critic discussing *The Good Glass of Beer*, a work that, for the first time in Manet's life, earned him unqualified public acclaim. Here was a 'type', a 'character', whose traditional image was reassuring. It was, in fact, a portrait of the engraver-lithographer Emille Bellot, a habitué of one of Manet's haunts, the Café Guerbois. Manet had just returned from Holland, and the work attests to the Frenchman's admiration for Frans Hals. As the Paris-based Belgian painter Alfred Stevens put it, '[Manet] drank the beer of Haarlem'.

'This year M. Manet has watered down his beer,' they could say. Perhaps he believed he had at long last been accepted and would henceforth be able to introduce modernity to the official Salon, rendering needless his participation in such other 'secessionist' exhibitions as that of the Impressionists.

'The Realist movement no longer needs to struggle with others. It is, it exists, it must show itself as independent. There must be a Realist Salon. Manet doesn't understand that. I think he is decidedly more conceited than intelligent.' Ironically, the person who held these strong views was one of Manet's closest friends: Degas. The relationship between the two contemporaries and social equals was close but often tumultuous.

Manet and Degas

Compared with the introverted, intellectual, misanthropic, worried Degas, Manet was confident and easy – as susceptible to praise and success as to failure, but always sure of his genius and brilliance. He was a celebrity of the streets, 'as well known as Garibaldi', noted Degas. He was also wilful. There is a popular anecdote about a present that Degas gave him, a portrait of Manet listening to Suzanne at the piano; Manet promptly ripped off the entire right side because he did not care for the rendering of his wife's face. 'How shocked I was when I saw my study at the Manets,' Degas later recalled. 'I left without saying goodbye, taking my painting with me. Once home, I took down a small still life [Manet] had given me. "Monsieur," I wrote him, "I send you back your plums!" ' But when asked whether the two painters ever saw each other again, Degas exclaimed, 'How can one remain on bad terms with Manet!'

Most of the time during those years, according to Berthe Morisot, the two men were inseparable. They were always arguing about who had been first in the modern movement, Degas reproaching Manet for having painted horse-racing scenes or 'women in the tub' and Manet retorting that Degas 'smelled of the Ecole [des Beaux-Arts]' and that he 'was painting Sémiramis when he [Manet] was painting modern Paris.'

Even if he did not often say it directly to Manet, Degas had great admiration for his friend's prodigious qualities as a painter. He bought a number of Manet's works after his death (Degas outlived Manet by

degas

more than thirty years), including a version of *The Execution of Maximilian,* which had also been cut up – this time by Manet's family – and which Degas personally restored, a poignant gesture when one remembers the other mutilated work.

● The face of Degas – Socrates, Homer – this mask with the sad gaze, so reflective, compare it with that of Manet, who, at fifty and ill, kept the smile of a successful politician with his charming courtesy.●

Jacques-Emile Blanche

Parisian landscapes

Manet and Degas had one trait in common that separated them from the group of Impressionists working at Argenteuil – Renoir, Sisley and Monet – and from those at Auvers-sur-Oise – Pissarro and Cézanne: their indifference to landscape. Like his friend, Manet was to the end a painter of people, even if he occasionally painted them out of doors, as he did in the

Degas (in the photograph opposite) made this wash drawing of Manet leaning against a wall (1866–8, left), as well as this painting (c. 1868–9, above) showing him listening to his wife at the piano. After Manet, who was unhappy with Degas' depiction of his wife, tore off a section of the work, Degas attached a new strip of canvas to it, no doubt planning to repaint it someday.

1870s. Also like Degas, Manet was first and foremost a man of the city.

Manet's painting *The Railway* (one must imagine the train having entered the station behind the models) is chiefly a portrait, the last that Manet would do of Victorine, looking altogether believable as a mother, enhanced by a dozing puppy on her knees; her bold gaze is attentive and participatory, but she appears indifferent to the white plumes of smoke just visible behind the iron bars that separate her from her industrial surroundings at the entrance of the Gare Saint-Lazare, whose wonderful modernity would soon inspire Monet's celebrated series of paintings.

In *The Laundry* (1875), Manet posed a young woman washing her clothes in a tub in a small garden in the Batignolles quarter. The jury of the Salon of 1876 was particularly set against this work because of its impudent application of two of the most frowned-upon practices of the day: the use of Impressionist techniques of rendering and the depiction of a naturalistic subject. In the eyes of the jury, the work was unnecessarily vulgar.

'Be truthful, let them say what they will'

Faced with the rejection of both *The Laundry* and *The Artist* – a portrait of a colourful habitué of the Café Guerbois, the painter and engraver Marcellin Desboutin – Manet decided to again invite the public to an unusual exhibition in his own studio at No. 4 Rue de Saint-Pétersbourg. The invitation carried the following message in gold letters: 'Be truthful, let them say what they will.' The crowds thronged – there were some four hundred visitors a day! – and the press made much of the event. Several articles gave accounts of the exhibition and described the studio and the artist: 'What! This man with fine features, placid gaze, blond and well-groomed beard, this man dressed in black, well-scrubbed, with good shirts and gloves, is the creator of the Boaters [*Argenteuil*]!';

Monsieur,

Vous avez bien voulu me demander d'être autorisé à faire dans un de nos dépôts, une étude d'après une machine locomotive montée par son mécanicien et son chauffeur.

After having requested authorization from the Compagnie des Chemins de Fer de l'Ouest to do a painting in one of its stations, Manet received a favourable response (some of which is printed here). But in 1881 he was already too sick and was unable to realize his idea of painting an engineer on top of a locomotive.

Did the caricaturists recognize the smouldering Olympia, maternal and dressed, ten years later? *The Railway* (1872–3, left) was the last portrait Manet made of his notorious muse Victorine Meurent.

'Seeing themselves painted this way, the unhappy ones wanted to flee! But M. Manet, in anticipation of this, has put up a barrier that prevents their escape.'

Cham

or, 'M. Manet belongs to that race of decorous revolutionaries, well-brought-up men of the world, like Robespierre or M. Louis Blanc' [socialist journalist]; or 'He…is paradox incarnate.'

Manet and Mallarmé

It was again a poet, Stéphane Mallarmé, who, in an article written in 1876 entitled 'The Impressionists and Edouard Manet' – originally published in London in English (but known to have been read by Manet) conferred the most resounding praise upon the painter, referring to him as the premier painter of light. According to Mallarmé, *The Laundry* was 'a work that was perhaps a turning point in an artistic career and was for certain in the history of art…. Everywhere, the atmosphere, luminous and transparent, is one with the figures, the clothes, the foliage, seeming to appropriate a little of their substance and of their solidity, while the contours, gnawn by the hidden sun and consumed by the space around them, tremble, melt and evaporate in the ambient air, which seems to hide their reality in order to preserve the authenticity of the figures. The air rules in absolute reality, as if possessing an enchanted existence, bestowed upon it through the sorcery of art.'

That same year, Manet made a portrait of Mallarmé about which Georges Bataille justly wrote that it 'radiated the friendship of two great minds'. It certainly suggests the affectionate attentions of Manet, who must have caught his young friend in a moment of intellectual reverie during the course of their daily conversations in his studio. 'I saw my dear Manet every day for ten years, and I find his absence today hard to believe,' the poet wrote in 1885, two years after Manet's death. Mallarmé has described Manet as 'freed from the worries of creation, [chattering] in the studio by the light of the lamps; this brilliant talker reveals what he meant by painting, the tidings of destiny that were reserved for him, and why

The painter and the poet Mallarmé, the latter Manet's junior by ten years, were very close. After leaving the Lycée Fontane (Condorcet), where he taught English, Mallarmé would spend a long time every evening in Manet's studio. Here is the portrait made of him in the fall of 1876. 'Sensitive to the artist's genius, he was no less so to the man's charm,' recalled Henri de Régnier. 'I heard him speak of Manet only with profound admiration and tender camaraderie.' Below is Manet's drawing illustrating his friend's *L'Après-midi d'un Faune* (1876).

and how he painted by irrepressible instinct.'

Mallarmé was a close observer of Manet's complex temperament, the extreme contrast between the apparent lightheartedness of the boulevardier and the almost fatal attraction he felt for a mode of painting so ill suited for the success he so fervently desired. It was Mallarmé who provided us with this famous elliptical portrait of Manet, which is at the same time so elliptical and so precise, each word carefully judged: 'Among the ruins, goat-footed, a virile innocence in a beige overcoat, beard and thin blond hair, greying with wit. At Tortoni's, an elegant scoffer; in the studio, a fury would seize him before the blank canvas – bewildered as though he had never before painted in his life.'

‘ The natural light of day, which penetrates and modifies everything, remaining invisible all the while, reigns over this exemplary work [*The Laundry*, 1875, opposite]…’

Stéphane Mallarmé

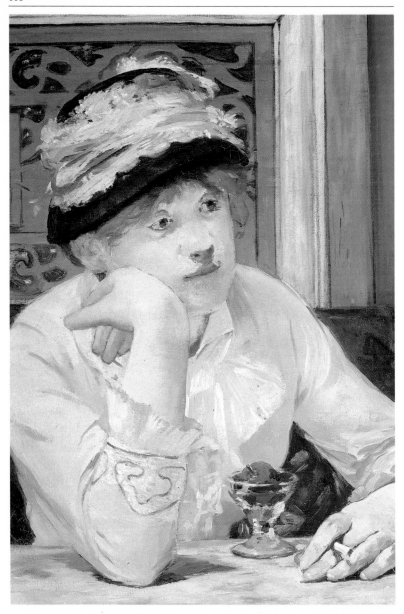

Manet, the man as much as the painter, incarnated glittering Paris at the end of the 19th century – its elegant boulevards, its wit and its civility, as well as its rebellious spirit and openness to the new, the instinctive rather than the theoretical. In conversation as in painting, he was lively and quick – not frivolous, but the opposite of heavy. And deft: he headed straight to his goal with just the right word or brush stroke.

CHAPTER 6

SCENES OF PARISIAN LIFE

Manet evidently gave in to a prank by the photographer Dallemagne, who framed him like a work of art (right). Opposite is a detail of *The Plum* (1878), a café scene for which an actress friend of Manet's posed in his studio.

'Concision in art is a necessity as well as an elegance,' Manet advised the young painter Jeanniot, adding these words, which reveal how distant he remained from orthodox Impressionism: 'Cultivate your memories; nature will never give you anything but hints – it's like a railing that keeps you from falling into banality. You must constantly remain the master and do as you please. No tasks! No, no tasks!…'

Manet the portraitist

Manet also gave the following advice to Jeanniot about portraiture: 'In a figure look for the highest light and the deepest shadow, the rest will come naturally.' These principles had already been observed in portraits of Victorine and Berthe Morisot, whose faces frequently look as if they had been lit by spotlights. This approach is typical of all the works he made from 1870 on, until shortly before his death.

This well-behaved child, posing for his father's friend, is the future playwright Henri Bernstein.

Manet regretted never receiving any formal commissions. He fretted and fumed against the aesthetic choices of his republican friends who finally came into power after 1872, and from whom he had hoped for more artistic tolerance. While it is true that the banker Marcel Bernstein asked Manet to paint his little boy in a sailor suit (Henri, the future dramatist), it was out of friendship rather than because of the painter's prestige. Manet did paint the portrait of the now very official Antonin Proust – France's Minister of Culture under Prime Minister Léon Gambetta in 1881–2 – but it was because he was his best friend

In the traditional painter's pose – imitating his dear Velázquez in *Las Meninas* – Manet kept his elegant hat on, though his brush is ready to put colour on his palette. Manet crudely sketched some details – the hand and the palette, for instance – in order to concentrate light and thought on the essentials: the eye, the brow and the brush lit from above – the fixed arrow ready to reach its mark.

from childhood. And it was Manet himself who asked Henri Rochefort and Georges Clemenceau (a future prime minister of France who was then a radical member of the Chamber of Deputies) if they would be willing to pose for him. Neither man appreciated the result, yet both likenesses are surprising for their insight and truthfulness. (André Malraux, France's minister of culture under Charles de Gaulle, was mistaken when – in his passion to see Manet as the inventor of pure painting and thus implicitly the destroyer of the subject in painting – he wrote 'for Manet to paint Clemenceau, he had to resolve to put himself entirely into it, and almost nothing of Clemenceau'.)

This astonishing portrait of Georges Clemenceau (1879–80, opposite), whose features – though spare – are powerfully expressive, apparently did not please its sitter. 'My portrait by Manet?' the future Prime Minister is reputed to have said. 'Very bad. I do not have it and therefore it does not bother me in the least. It is at the Louvre, and I myself wonder why they put it there!'

Women

Manet loved to paint women far more than he did politicians. More often than not, he showed them disguised, playing roles, recording their gestures as social

archetypes. Early in his career, he had dressed the photographer Nadar's mistress in masculine Spanish costume and his own model Victorine as a toreador. In the 1870s, he proposed the portrait of the elegant Madame Guillemet, seated on a bench next to her husband in a jungle-like winter garden, like the one on whose eroticism Zola had just elaborated in a famous scene in *La Curée* (*The Female Vicar*, 1872).

For *The Plum* (1878), Manet re-created a café decor in the studio. His friend the actress Ellen Andrée posed for it (two years earlier, Andrée had been the model for Degas' *Absinthe*). A key compositional element, Andrée's fresh complexion is by no means that of an alcoholic! On the contrary, Manet delights in the savoury pinks of the flesh and her dress. Degas' *Absinthe* is a social statement; *The Plum*, the depiction of a delectable reverie. The woman in *The Lady with the Fans*, disguised as an Algerian

The actress Ellen Andrée (photograph below) enjoyed sitting for her painter friends. In *The Plum* (1878, opposite below), Manet put her in the naturalistic and very Parisian role of a young woman, perhaps a little tipsy, waiting in a café.

and set against a Japanese background, was Nina de Callias, an accomplished pianist whose musical, literary and artistic salons were among the most brilliant in Paris.

Méry Laurent was Manet's closest woman friend during his last years. A lavishly kept woman, she loved to surround herself with luxury, but also with painters and writers, the most smitten being Mallarmé. Manet was enchanted with her gaiety, her health and her

In *In The Conservatory* (1879, above and details opposite), Manet painted the portrait of a bourgeois couple, updating a traditional genre. The focus is on the two hands, duly ringed.

For this painting (1879–80, left), the singer Emilie Ambre posed as Carmen, her favourite operatic role. Full of enthusiasm for Manet's paintings, she decided, on her first opera tour in 1879–80, to take *The Execution of Maximilian* to the United States, where it was rather coldly received. Above is a sketch in watercolour done on graph paper in about 1880, doubtless rendered on the spot in a café.

elegance, and often painted her dressed in furs, her head covered with a toque or a large hat.

Pastels

During the last two years of his life, when illness made it difficult for him to undertake large works, Manet produced numerous small still lifes of fruits and flowers, but mainly he liked to make pastel portraits of his women visitors, pastel being a medium that was less tiring to work with and more rapid than oil.

He thus immortalized the various charms of Irma Brunner, 'the lovely Viennese', and the Valtesse de la Bigne – women who lived off their charms; Madame Guillemet, who ran a business selling fancy lingerie; actresses such as Emilie Ambre and Jeanne Demarsy; and young sophisticates such as Suzette Lemaire, the daughter of a painter friend, and Isabelle Lemonnier, the sister-in-law of Georges Charpentier, a publisher of the naturalist writers and future champion of the Impressionists.

'Since...1878, Manet suffered attacks of illness and constant emotional upset,' attested his friend Pierre Prins, 'though his spirits never flagged...it is odd, but the presence of a woman, no matter who she was, would help him regain his composure'.

During the summer of 1880, Isabelle Lemonnier – one of Manet's favourite models – received a series of illustrated letters from the painter. The image on the left is from one in which he imagines her diving. Below is her likeness from another letter.

Overleaf: Manet's elegant friends Irma Brunner (1880?, left) and Méry Laurent (1882, right).

First dealer, first collector

The dealer Paul Durand-Ruel, who had earlier been a specialist in the Barbizon School, 'discovered' the paintings of Monet and Pissarro in London, where the two had sought refuge during the Franco-Prussian war of 1870. In January 1872, when he visited the studio of Alfred Stevens in Paris – a successful society painter but also a very good friend to the Impressionists – Durand-Ruel had been particularly impressed by two of Manet's works from the 1860s – *Still Life with Salmon* and *Moonlight at Boulogne* – which Manet had left with his friend to attract a future buyer. (Until then, Manet had never really sold anything, although ten years had elapsed since his first success at the Salon.) The dealer became interested in the painter, and the next day returned to buy twenty-two of his works. Henceforth, it would be Durand-Ruel who would be his chief advocate.

114

The principal collector of Manet's work while he was alive was neither a banker nor a wealthy bourgeois, but a man of the stage who had become famous and well-to-do. And, like Manet, he was a boulevardier. This was the baritone singer Jean-Baptiste

Faure. Faure possessed as many as sixty-seven works by Manet, among them *The Spanish Singer, Mlle V... in the Costume of an Espada, Le Déjeuner sur l'Herbe, Lola of Valencia, The Fifer* and *The Railway*. The era of Moreau-Nélaton and the Havemeyers – the two names we associate today with major collections of Manet's paintings – and public subscriptions for Manet's work was yet to come.

Jean-Baptiste Faure, the celebrated opera singer and collector of Manet's works, is shown here in a photograph and in an 1877 work by Manet from the ghost scene in *Hamlet*.

Stage portrait

In 1877 Manet painted a portrait of Faure in the title role of Ambroise Thomas' opera *Hamlet*, the vehicle that had secured his celebrity status in 1868. Manet chose the most dramatic moment: the apparition of the ghost before Hamlet's hallucinating eyes.

In this work, Manet rediscovered the powerful blacks of his Spanish-style paintings of the previous decade, contrasting them with the harshly lit face illuminated by the stage footlights. It is one of the rare portraits where Manet – usually preferring tranquillity, if not downright indifference and vacancy, in the faces of his models – allowed a hint of expression to emerge.

'After having posed twenty times,' Faure recollected, 'I was obliged to leave to sing I don't know where.... Upon my return I found that the portrait had been altogether altered, with a blinking supernatural ground and legs that were no longer my own.

'These are not my legs,' I told him, surprised that my image only half suited. 'What does it matter to you!' [Manet replied,] 'I took them from a model who has finer ones than yours!' After a sourish correspondence, we became friends as back in the old days.... Because of him, I threw my lot with the intransigents in the matter of painting. He sent me Degas, Pissarro, Sisley, Claude Monet, from all of whom I acquired so many works.' This anecdote reveals many facets of Manet's character: his sense of freedom as a painter; the irrepressibly offhand manner with which he treated his only collector – of whose vanity he was certainly aware; his mocking wit; and, finally, his exceptional generosity towards his younger colleagues.

The critics and the cartoonists had a field day when the painting *Faure in the Role of Hamlet* was shown at the Salon of 1877. 'The king of the intransigents wanted to make a portrait of the king of singers. The portrait is ridiculous,' stated one. Drawings by Cham carried the captions like 'Hamlet, gone crazy, has himself painted by M. Manet' and 'A portrait of a tadpole'. This anonymous caricature (above) was accompanied by a pithy text: 'M. Faure shrunk by M. Manet.' The poor Faure must have suffered, though this makes his merit as a collector all the greater!

Masks and costumes

One of the first paintings Faure bought of Manet's was *Masked Ball at the Opéra,* painted in the spring of 1873, the very year that this opera house on the Rue Le Pelletier, where Degas had also worked a good deal, disappeared in a fire.

It was a specific event Manet depicted – the famous annual masked ball, which took place at the end of March. There is no doubt that Manet was in attendance, but he associated it with a particular memory: the scenery of the first act of the naturalistic play by the Goncourt brothers, *Henriette Maréchal.* (This play had caused a scandal in 1865, the same year that the

Olympia did; it, too, was accused of vaunting a vulgar 'modern realism'.)

As in *Music in the Tuileries Gardens,* Manet introduced a few of his friends in this frieze of men-about-town in top hats, whom he had pose in his new studio on the Rue d'Amsterdam, in the heart of Paris. 'The solitude where he had lived and worked came to an end,' recalled Théodore Duret. 'He received more frequent visits from a large number of men and women who made up Parisian society, who, drawn by his renown and the pleasure of his company, came to see him and, on occasion, agreed to serve as his models.'

Thus it was that the author of these words posed for this painting, along with the collector Albert Hecht, the composer Emmanuel Chabrier, an intimate of Manet's and his wife's, and a few other now-forgotten painters. The identity of the 'female dominoes' (masked women)

M *asked Ball at the Opéra* (1873–4) is more suggestive of a funeral than the expected devilish swirl, even though Manet made at least one preparatory sketch (above left) on the spot at Rue Le Pelletier.

or the scantily clad Columbines decked out in seductive accessories is not known – all that is visible of one astride the balustrade at the top of the painting is her red boot. The contrast of the funereal garb worn by the men and the touches of colour on the women and the harlequin must have amused Manet and recall Gautier's contemporary lines: 'Carnival clowns the garb now emulate/Wherein we grace the ball, and go to a funeral.'

• The costumes merely break up the monotony of the background of black frock coats with some fresh floral tones.•
Stéphane Mallarmé

Heroines of modern Paris

Since *Masked Ball at the Opéra* was deemed too naturalistic by the jury of the 1874 Salon, one should not be surprised to learn that in 1877 the jury also rejected *Nana*. This work was a full-length portrait of the type of woman to be found at the ball. If *Olympia* was perceived to be a Baudelairean prostitute, *Nana* was a contemporary tart, very Third Republic. She was painted during the winter of 1876–7, more than three years before the publication of Zola's novel of the same name. The work was no doubt named thus the moment Manet presented it to the Salon, as soon as Manet had learned of the title of the forthcoming novel of his erstwhile champion. 'Manet was absolutely right to present us in his *Nana* one of the most perfect examples of this type of girl that his friend, our dear master, Emile Zola, is going to portray for us in one of his forthcoming novels,' novelist Joris-Karl Huysmans declared.

Nonetheless, Manet's *Nana* is different from Zola's: Zola's character is clearly a vamp, while Manet's is simply a big-hearted girl who seems to like showing off in her corset, shaking her powder-puff. And so she was! Manet had one of his friends pose, the actress Henriette Hauser, a woman who was well known to all of Parisian gallant society. Once more, he had provoked the jury. Hauser appears again in 1877, in a scene of a popular Parisian diversion: *Skating*. Here she is an elegant and stout visitor to the newest fashionable spectacle on the Champs-Elysées. Through his rough technique, Manet attempted to evoke from memory in his studio the nocturnal, fluttering spectacle and the whirling movement of the crowd and the skaters.

Café-concerts

Among the prominent places Manet frequented were the cafés, restaurants and music-halls where artists, writers

For *Nana* (1877, opposite) and *Skating* (1877, below), Manet asked the actress and demimondaine Henriette Hauser to pose. In one work she is a spectator at the edge of the skating rink on the Champs-Elysées; in the other, she

mimes a scene from a courtesan's life. This last work, deemed indecent, was turned down by the jury of the 1877 Salon, an act that prompted these words from Manet, recollected by Antonin Proust: 'Nymphs offering themselves to satyrs is all right. A pretty woman in her underclothes is forbidden!' He showed *Nana* in the window of a store on the Boulevard des Capucines, where she nearly provoked riots.

In *Nana*, thus baptized in 1877, well before the famous novel by Zola appeared in 1880, Manet repeated the theme of the courtesan, which had caused such a scandal with *Olympia* – only this time he chose a style that was closer to the naturalistic literature of the time. It may have been a sentence from Zola's *L'Assommoir* (published that year), in which Nana is first introduced as an adolescent, that inspired Manet: 'Since the morning, she had spent hours in her chemise before the bit of looking glass hanging above the bureau…she had the fine fragrance of youth, the bare skin of a child and of a woman.'

and society people and the demimonde liked to go to see and be seen. These were places of pleasure and of lovers' meetings, but they also functioned as centres of intellectual and artistic exchange. 'I attended neither Oxford nor Cambridge,' recalled the young Irish artist George Moore, who was in Paris during those years, 'but I attended the Nouvelle-Athènes…the Académie des Beaux-Arts. No, not the official institution, but the real Académie Française: the Café.'

During the 1870s, a tacit sharing of analogous subjects took place between Degas and Manet. Degas showed the active Paris, that of movement and work – the world of dancers, musicians, milliners, prostitutes, acrobats, laundresses and other people who were not at all from his own class. Manet, on the other hand, usually chose to

reflect a more familiar, more frivolous world, men and
women in moments of relaxation, gaiety, nonchalance,
in search of small quotidian pleasures – out for an
afternoon of rowing (*Boating*), drinking
beer or listening to music (*At the Café, Girl
Serving Beer*), flirting at a restaurant table
(*At Père Lathuille's Restaurant*), reading a
newspaper (*Reading*), or, as in his final
masterpiece, *A Bar at the Folies-Bergère,*
simply waiting for a customer.

To each his genius: Degas' eye was
searching; that of Manet registered the
particular places of those slightly vulgar
modern manners of the boulevard by using
his sparkling wit, his admirable qualities as
a painter and his innate kindness towards
others – 'his tender scepticism', as his
biographer Jacques-Emile Blanche would
say – to produce icons of modern life.

*A*t the Café (above),
at a café-concert,
and at a café (above left).

G eorge Moore at a
café, which he called
'the real Académie
Française'.

At the Folies-Bergère

In the winter of 1877–8, Manet had begun
a large work for the Salon that depicted the
Reishoffen Brasserie, a café-concert located between
the Boulevard de Rochechouart and the Place Clichy.
For reasons that are not known – though, as we have
seen, Manet had already cut up other major works – he

divided this canvas into two parts and renamed them. The one on the right became *Girl Serving Beer,* the other, *At the Café.* Perhaps Manet, the great simplifier, had the impression that too many figures would dissipate the viewer's attention? If this was the case, he neatly avoided this stumbling block in his last great work, *A Bar at the Folies-Bergère,* painted during the winter of 1881–2, when he was already very handicapped by the disease (syphilitic locomotor ataxia) that would eventually cause his death.

For once it was not one of his women friends whom he asked to pose (two of them, however, can be discerned

For Manet, Père Lathuille's, a garden restaurant on the Avenue de Clichy, had the advantage of allowing him to paint simultaneously a scene of Parisian life and figures out of doors.

in the balcony: Méry Laurent in white and Jeanne Demarsy with the twins). No, this time, he borrowed a real serving girl from a bar at the Folies-Bergère. She came to pose in his studio, in front of a reconstituted bar on which he had placed a sumptuous still life of fruits, flowers and bottles. The purpose of the mirror was to reflect the sparkling ambience of this café-concert, a pastime then very much in fashion, albeit slightly debauched – 'the only place in Paris that stinks so

Taken at about the time Manet was executing his famous painting, this photograph is of the café-concert at the Folies-Bergère, a place known for its acrobatic spectacles and easy social intercourse.

sweetly of the maquillage of purchased favours and the extremes of jaded corruption' (Huysmans). The serving girl, who was shown alone from the front – and, strangely, also from behind in the mirror – appears to be holding a conversation with a customer. Her flesh and bouquet of roses are like offerings, as if at the summit of the pyramid of the things to be tasted on the counter. She counters all of this potential temptation with a gaze that is both weary and absent. There is something poignant in this quintessential image of the Parisian universe that had been Manet's life, his world. The party was over. Farewell my beauty, farewell to life. Farewell to painting.

Manet chose to show not the crowd at the Folies-Bergère, but one of the three bars of the circular promenade,

A lively studio

During his final years, when he was finishing *A Bar*, all of Paris filed through his studio, the atmosphere of which Blanche later described: '[Composer] Emmanuel Chabrier would make up sayings. Manet adored puns, something that has so much gone out of fashion. By five o'clock it was barely possible to find a seat next to the artist. On a small round iron table, which often appears

described by Guy de Maupassant in his story *Bel-Ami* (1885): 'A group of women awaited arrivals at one or another of three bars behind which, heavily made up and wilting, three vendors of refreshments and love held court.'

The serving girl's back in *A Bar at the Folies-Bergère* has generated a lot of speculation. Judging from her reflection in the mirror – in which one is able to see almost the entire crowded room – she is leaning towards a man who has no doubt given his order for a drink from the bar. Seen from the front, however, she seems to be more vertical and to be looking rather dejectedly at us, not her customer; in reality, the man reflected in the glass would hide her from our view. 'M. Manet's *A Bar at the Folies-Bergère* bewilders the throng of visitors, who exchange puzzled comments concerning the mirage of this canvas… which is not quite right optically. The subject is modern enough…but what is the meaning of this lighting? Gas light, electric light? Not at all, it is a vague *plein-air*, a bath of wan daylight,' wrote Huysmans. The faulty perspective and this aura of unreality were deliberate. They were the result of Manet having painted the girl – and the table and still life in front of her – in daylight in his studio, all the while superimposing the memory of the nighttime scene on his daytime observations.

in Manet's work, a waiter served mugs of beer and
apéritifs. The frequenters of the boulevard would come
to keep their comrade company – who could no longer
go down to the Café de Bade…. After laborious, though
short, sessions, Manet, who tired quickly, would stretch
out on the low couch against the light of the window
and contemplate what he had just finished painting,
twisting his moustache and gesturing like a kid saying:
"Nice, very nice!" The others would laugh and pretend
to be the furious jury of the Salon rejecting his work.
Manet no longer fretted about this, since by then "his
name was a flag"; he was the head of a school without a
school. He was supported by a party that used him as
one would a candidate to sign revolutionary manifestoes
during the run-up to an election as a stalking-horse for
others "less extreme". … His "defective" masterpieces lay
gathering dust, in a cupboard where no one imagined
turning them over, because one only went to see him for
conversation. It was thought (by Zola, at any rate)

Manet sent this
illustrated letter
(1880, above) to Isabelle
Lemonnier offering her
a drawing of a fruit from
his garden accompanied
by a poem he wrote in
her honour.

that he was searching for something…that others with
more talent would find…. The "defects" that separated
him from the public were his essential qualities, the
"fatality" of his gift.'

'Greater than we thought'

The pallbearers at Manet's funeral, which took place on
3 May 1883, were Antonin Proust, Emile Zola, Philippe
Burty, Alfred Stevens, Théodore Duret and Claude
Monet. His old comrades from Montmartre were all
there, painters of every bent. Degas followed Manet's
funeral procession to the cemetery. 'He was greater than
we thought,' he said.

Manet died at the age of fifty-one. His career as an
artist had lasted scarcely more than twenty years, during
which time his boisterous public image and his charm
eclipsed his greatness as a painter, even in the opinion of
the greatest thinkers. The noise of the boulevard died
down. Slowly, the accolades began.

Overleaf: sick and
reclusive during the
last year of his life, Manet
was able to execute only
pastel portraits and still
lifes of fruits and flowers,
which were then often
given away to his friends.
In the summer of 1882,
the painter made
spectacular use of the
last roses and tulips in his
garden at Rueil, placing
them in a glass decorated
with a dragon.

DOCUMENTS

Meetings with Manet

Everyone agreed that Manet was seduction itself. But his charm, his wit, his gaiety and the elegance with which he hid his torments and his artistic obsessions could overshadow his genius as a painter.

Early years

Antonin Proust, Manet's oldest friend, quickly abandoned painting to become a journalist and a politician. Proust was Léon Gambetta's secretary, and then his minister of fine arts for a few months during the winter of 1881–2 when Gambetta was premier of France. Manet painted Proust's portrait, portraying him as a very official personage, in 1880.

Manet was of average height and very muscular. His straight back and his rhythmic gait gave his presence a special elegance. Though he often exaggerated his postures and affected the drawling speech of a Paris urchin, he was never vulgar. You sensed his breeding.

Beneath a broad forehead, his nose plunged straight down, while his mouth curved up at the corners, giving him a teasing expression. His glance was bright, and his eyes, though small, darted around the place.

When he was quite young, he would fling back a head of long, naturally curly hair. At seventeen his hairline was already receding, but his beard had grown, blurring the contour of his lips and leaving bare a smooth white chin. The lower part of his face softened, harmonizing with the fine greying hair that framed his forehead. Few men have been so attractive.

Despite his wit and his tendency to scepticism, he remained naive. He was surprised by everything and was amused by anything. On the other hand, he took anything to do with art very seriously. On this point, he was intractable. He would not alter his understanding. He would allow neither contradiction nor even discussion.

Antonin Proust
Edouard Manet, Souvenirs
1897

Manet in Spain, 1865

In 1865, after the scandal of the Olympia, *Manet was deeply crushed and made a journey to Spain. It is there that he met Théodore Duret, the man who was to become one of his closest friends as well as his biographer.*

When the Salon was closed in the month of August, in order to secure a brief respite from persecution, he carried out his long matured project of a visit to Madrid. It was there that I made his acquaintance. The manner of our meeting was so remarkable and so typical of his impulsive character that I feel bound to relate the incident here.

I was returning from Portugal, through which I had travelled partly on horseback, and had arrived that very morning from Badajoz, after [rushing] for forty hours. A new hotel had just been opened in Madrid, in the Puerta del Sol, on the model of the large European hotels – a thing hitherto unknown in Spain. I arrived worn out with fatigue and literally famishing of hunger. The new hotel where I had put up appeared to me a veritable palace of delight. The lunch to which I had sat down seemed like a feast of Lucullus. I ate with a sensation of luxury. The dining hall was empty except for a gentleman who was sitting some distance away at the same long table as myself. He, however, found the cuisine execrable. Every other minute he ordered some new dish, which immediately afterwards he angrily rejected as inedible. Each time that he sent the waiter away, I on the contrary called him back, and with ravenous appetite partook of all the dishes indifferently. Meanwhile I had paid no attention to my neighbour who was so difficult to please. When, however, I again asked the waiter to bring me a dish which he had refused, he suddenly got up, came near to where I was sitting and exclaimed angrily. 'Now, sir, you are doing this simply to insult me, to make a fool of me – pretending to relish this disgusting cooking and calling back the waiter every time that I send him away!' The profound astonishment that I displayed at this unexpected attack immediately convinced him that he must have made a mistake as to the motive of my behaviour, for he added in a milder tone, 'You recognize me; of course, you know who I am?'

Still more astonished, I replied, 'I don't know who you are. How should I recognize you? I have just arrived from Portugal. I nearly perished of hunger there, and the cuisine of this hotel seemed to me to be really excellent.' 'Ah, you have come from Portugal,' he said, 'well, I've just come from Paris.' This at once explained our divergence of opinion as to the cooking. Realising the humour of the situation, my friend began to laugh at his fit of anger, and then made his apologies. We drew our chairs nearer to one another and finished our lunch together.

Afterwards he told me his name. He confessed that he had supposed that I was some one who had recognized him and wished to play a vulgar joke upon him. The idea that the persecution which he thought he had escaped by leaving Paris was about to begin again in Madrid had at once exasperated him. The acquaintance thus begun rapidly kindled into intimacy. We explored Madrid together. Naturally we spent a considerable time every day before the paintings of Velázquez in the Prado. At this time Madrid preserved its old picturesque appearance. There was still a number of cafés in the old houses of the Calle di Sevilla, which formed a general rendezvous for people connected with bull-fighting, toreros, aficionados and for dancers. Large awnings were stretched across the street from the upper storeys of the houses, giving it an agreeable shade and comparative coolness in the afternoon. The Calle di Sevilla with its picturesque life became our favourite haunt. We saw several bull-fights – Manet made sketches of them, which he used later for his paintings. We also went to

At the Prado, an etching after Goya.

Toledo to see the Cathedral and Greco's pictures. There is no need to tell how everything that Manet saw in Spain, which had haunted his dreams for so long, fulfilled his utmost expectations. One thing, however, spoilt his pleasure – the difficulty which he had experienced from the first, of accommodating himself to the Spanish mode of living. He could not fall in with it. He almost gave up eating. He felt an overpowering repugnance to the odour of the dishes that were set before him. He was in fact a Parisian who could find no comfort out of Paris. At the end of ten days, really starved and ill, he was obliged to return.

Théodore Duret
Manet, translated by
J. E. Crawford Flitch, 1937

At the Manets, 1869–70

The Manets and the Morisots quickly became good friends. Mme Morisot went with her daughters to the Thursday evenings hosted by Mme Auguste Manet, which were attended by Edouard, his wife, Suzanne, and his brothers, Eugène and Gustave. There one met Baudelaire, Degas, [the poet] Charles Cros, Zola, Astruc, and Stevens at whose home one made the acquaintance of Puvis de Chavannes. Bosc sang, accompanying himself on the guitar. Emmanuel Chabrier played with an unbridled exuberance the *Danse Macabre* of Saint-Saëns. Mme Edouard Manet had a particular way of interpreting Chopin, her little hands with a light touch on the piano; there was a great deal of discussion....

After Denis Rouart
Berthe Morisot

At the vernissage of the Salon of 1869

You will understand that my first concern was to make my way to Gallery 'M'. I found Manet, his hat over his eyes, looking bewildered; he begged me to look at his painting since he dare not himself. I have never seen such an expressive face. He laughed uneasily, declaring at one and the same time that his painting was very bad and that it would be very successful.

To me he is a decidedly charming person who pleases me immensely. His paintings, as usual, give the impression of strange, or even unripe, fruit. To me they are far from unpleasant. In the *Balcony* I am more odd than ugly. It seems that the epithet of 'femme fatale' has gone the rounds of the sightseers.

Berthe Morisot
Letter to her sister Edma
Morisot-Pontillon, 2 May 1869

Laughing with Manet

Your life strikes me as charming at this point...chatting with Degas while watching him sketch, laughing with Manet, philosophizing with Puvis, strike me as things worthy of envy.

Edma Morisot-Pontillon
Letter to her sister Berthe Morisot

At the café

George Moore, an Irish critic and novelist (1852–1933), came to Paris in 1873 to study painting, which he abandoned around 1876 to take up writing. His recollections of artistic Paris at the time are valuable. He very much admired Manet and worked actively to have his work known in Britain.

At that moment the glass door of the café grated upon the sanded floor, and Manet entered. Although by birth and by art essentially Parisian, there was something in his appearance and manner of speaking that often suggested an Englishman. Perhaps it was his dress – his clean-cut clothes and figure. That figure! those square shoulders that swaggered as he went across a room and the thin waist; and that face, the beard and nose, satyr-like shall I say? No, for I would evoke an idea of beauty of line united to that of intellectual expression – frank words, frank passion in his convictions, loyal and simple phrases, clear as well-water, sometimes a little hard, sometimes, as they flowed away, bitter, but at the fountain head sweet and full of light. He sits next to Degas, that round-shouldered man in suit of pepper and salt.... These two men are the leaders of the impressionist school.

George Moore
Confessions of a Young Man, 1972

At the Cirque Fernando, 1876

The Cirque Fernando was frequented by painters who were taken by such spectacles of modern life. Degas made a famous painting of it in 1879 (Mlle La La at the Cirque Fernando), as did Toulouse-Lautrec in 1888 and Seurat in 1890–1.

This Manet, with his small head à la Henri III, the most seductive and witty of men, the one with the finest soul, M. Gervex told us.… Our first meeting? Let me see…1876 – I was twenty-four years old. It took place at the Cirque Fernando, the actual Médrano, two steps away from the Nouvelle Athènes Café where the painters taken with reality and the outdoors would meet. Manet, my elder by twenty years, was in the company of Chavannes and of Degas. He introduced me to them as the creator of *The Autopsy at the Hôtel-Dieu*, which they had seen at the Salon. Manet spoke to me congenially.

Henri Gervex
'Souvenirs sur Manet'
Bulletin de la vie artistique
15 October 1920

Meeting in the Batignolles

One evening in October 1878, I was walking down the Rue Pigalle, when I saw coming towards me a man of youthful appearance, most distinguished, dressed with elegant simplicity. Fair hair, a light silky beard, grey eyes, a straight nose, flaring nostrils, gloved hands, a quick and springy step. It was Manet. I recognized him from his photograph, which had appeared in the *Galerie des Contemporains*.

I don't know what prevented me

from going up to him and expressing my admiration for him.… It was around six o'clock. I followed him for some time.… A little later, when I knew him, I told him how I had shadowed him admiringly. 'I am sorry that you didn't come up to me,' he told me, 'it would have given me pleasure to know another partisan in the army!' (The young painter was then doing his military service).

Manet was very successful at the Salon of 1880. The jury was unsure, however, whether to award him a second medal, and in the end, did not give it to him.

Georges Jeanniot
'En souvenir de Manet'
La Grande Revue
10 August 1907

At the Louvre: 'He said nothing and I heard everything'

Manet never found the time to paint Gambetta's portrait.

One morning when he was expressing his annoyance about his setback, we decided to distract him, to go to the office of Ronchaud, who at the time was the Louvre's director. There, Manet silently leafed through a collection of drawings by Filippo Lippi, Botticelli, Perugino, Mantegna and Carpaccio, among others.

'I am indebted to you', he told Gambetta while leaving, 'for having spent one of the most delightful mornings of my life. It seemed to me that I was as much with them as with you.'

'My own joy', retorted Gambetta, 'was above all to have brought you pleasure, my dear friend.'

* His hair and beard are light chestnut brown;
his eyes, narrow and deep set, have a boyish
liveliness and fire; his mouth very characteristic,
thin, mobile, a trifle mocking at the corners.*
Emile Zola

We left Manet on the Place Saint-Germain-l'Auxerrois.

'It would be impossible for me to imagine', Gambetta told me, 'anything more eloquent than Manet's eye, leafing through those drawings in that collection at the Louvre. He said nothing and I heard everything.'

Antonin Proust
Edouard Manet, Souvenirs
1897

Manet ill

The painter and engraver Pierre Prins had been close to Manet since the 1860s. He married Fanny Claus, the young violinist on the right of The Balcony.

Ever since the first attack of paralysis that had knocked him down in his studio in 1878, Manet suffered attacks, and constant emotional upset, especially when he was alone. It was then that he felt 'done for'. An expression of his that I heard I don't know how many times, he was so haunted by it. It is odd, but the presence of a woman, no matter who she was, would help him to regain his composure. Poor Suzanne had a lot to put up with....

The tale that he told to his family – that he had been the victim of a snakebite on the foot in the Brazilian forest during his trip there when he was eighteen years old – no longer held up. The ataxia that had manifested itself by then had an origin that was all too recognizable.... Too subtle to let himself be taken in by kind words, he was too nervous and too clairvoyant not to bitterly suffer the defeat that he dreaded. He felt first off struck down in his art and that was the hardest thing of all.... His brush 'disobeyed'!... Anguished, feverish in front of his canvas, undermined to his core.... How could one overcome that? His moodiness has been mentioned. I witnessed it...but he suffered it more than anyone. Then he would isolate himself 'like a sick cat', he said...rather than display his weakness.

Pierre Prins recalled by his son in
P. Prins, 1949

Manet's writings

Manet was not one of those painter-writers who leave behind their private diaries or theoretical treatises. His letters are lively and charming, but they never discuss his work. On the other hand, he spoke a great deal, and his remarks were documented by his friends and by journalists.

From an 1880 letter to Mme Guillemet.

From Rio de Janeiro to his mother, when he was seventeen

5 February 1849

Dear Maman,

We have finally anchored at Rio after two months at sea and a lot of bad weather....

The city is fairly big, though the streets are rather small; for a European who is somewhat artistic they offer a particular cachet; one doesn't meet in the street anyone but negroes and negresses; the Brazilian men go out little and the Brazilian women even less;... In this country, all the negroes are slaves; all these wretched ones look as if they had been brutalized; the power the whites have over them is extraordinary; I saw a slave market, it was a revolting spectacle; the negroes' outfit is limited to trousers, sometimes a cloth jacket, but because they are slaves, they aren't allowed to wear shoes. The negresses are for the most part naked to the waist, some of them have a scarf tied around their neck and draped over their chest, they are generally ugly, though I saw some who were rather pretty... Some of them wear turbans, others arrange their hair set in tight curls very artistically, and almost all wear skirts with enormous flounces.

As for the Brazilian women, they are generally very pretty; they have magnificent black eyes and similarly dark hair...they never go out alone, they are always followed by a negress or they are accompanied by their children....

We were unable to find a drawing master in Rio; thus, our commander urged me to give lessons to my comrades, so now I am elevated to the post of drawing master; it must be said that during the crossing I made myself

After his trip to Spain, Manet made these etchings based on Velázquez paintings.

such a reputation that each of the officers and teachers asked me for a likeness, and the commander even asked for his as a gift. I was delighted to fulfil all requests, so that everyone was pleased.

Your respectful son,
Edouard Manet

From Spain to Fantin-Latour, summer 1865

I *am* sorry that you aren't here, for what joy you would have to see Velázquez, who, alone, is worth the trip. The painters from every school, who fill the Museum of Madrid and who are well represented there, all seem fakers next to him. He is the painter of painters. He didn't surprise me, though he enthralled me. The full-length portrait that we have at the Louvre is not his. Only the Infanta cannot be contested....

The most astonishing piece of this splendid work, perhaps the most astonishing piece of painting that has ever been achieved, is the work shown in the catalogue: *Portrait of a Famous Actor at the Time of Philip IV.* The background disappears. It's just air that surrounds the man, all dressed in black and animated. And *The Weavers*, the beautiful portrait of Alonzo Cano, *Las Meninas...*an extraordinary work as well! The philosophers, what extraordinary pieces! All the dwarfs; one above all, seated frontally, his fists on his hips: a choice painting for a true connoisseur. His magnificent portraits; you would have to list all of them; there are only masterpieces....

And Goya! All the more strange compared with the master [Velázquez] whom he imitated too much, in the sense of the most servile imitation. Even so, a great liveliness. There are two beautiful equestrian portraits of his at the museum, done in the manner of Velázquez; rather inferior all the same. What I have seen of him so far hasn't pleased me enormously. I have to see in the coming days, a magnificent collection of his work at the Duke of Ossuna's.

I am sorry the weather is rather vile this morning, and I fear that the bullfight that should take place this evening, which I am looking forward to attending, will be put off. And then? Tomorrow, I go to Toledo. There, I will see El Greco and Goya, who are very well represented, so I have been told.

Madrid is a pleasant city, full of distractions. The Prado, a charming walk, is covered in pretty women, all in mantillas, which give them a unique look. In the streets, there are many costumes: the bullfighters also have an odd city costume.

To Suzanne Manet during the siege of Paris, 1870

23 October 1870

The newspapers have just announced that on Friday the Parisian army made a major attack on the enemy positions. They fought all day long. I think the Prussians have lost a lot of lives. On our side the losses are less considerable, even though poor Cuvelier, Degas' friend, was killed, and Leroux was wounded and, I think, taken prisoner. We're starting to get fed up with being quarantined and deprived of all communication, since it's been a month since we've had any news from you....

For a long time, my dear Suzanne, I was looking for your photograph. I finally found it in the album on the table in the sitting room and I can sometimes look at your pleasant face. Last night I awoke thinking that your

Q *ueue at the Butcher Shop*, an etching from 1870–1.

voice was calling me. The people who have remained in Paris see each other very little. We have become enormously selfish…. Otherwise every day we await some great event that will break the iron barrier that surrounds us. We count very much on the province

because we cannot massacre the little army that we have. Those Prussian rascals are capable of taking us by letting us starve. I had asked to be the attaché to the staff of General Vinoy. I wasn't able to obtain the post. I am sorry about it, as I would have been able to assist in all their operations….

Farewell, my dear Suzanne.

With love.

From Paris to Eva Gonzalès

19 November 1870

Dear Mademoiselle Eva,

One of our besieged friends asked me lately how I endured your absence, since the admiration and friendship I hold for you is of such public renown. Allow me to answer you directly… of all the deprivations this siege imposes upon us one of the most serious is that I am no longer able to see you…for two months I haven't had news from my poor Suzanne, who must be very worried although I write to her frequently – we are all soldiers here…. Degas and I are in the artillery as voluntary gunners. I am counting that on your return you will do my portrait with my large artilleryman's cloak. Tissot was glorious in the Jonchères affair, Jacquemart was there, Leroux was seriously wounded at Versailles, the poor Cuvelier killed; my brothers [and] Guillemet are in the battalions of the National Guard and are just waiting to go the front lines…. My soldier's kit is filled with my paintbox, my country easel, everything I need so that no time is lost and so I will be able to benefit from the facilities that I find everywhere. Many cowards have left, alas, among them our friends Zola, Fantin, etc…. I think I will give them a hard time on their return.

From Paris to Berthe Morisot

10 June 1871

Dear Mademoiselle,

We have been back in Paris for a few days and the ladies have asked me to convey my greetings to you and Mme Pontillon, where you are no doubt staying.

What terrible events [the Commune and the repression of the Commune]! How are we going to get through them? Everyone is transferring the blame on to his neighbour. In fact, we have all been party to what has taken place…. Here we are all on the verge of ruin; we shall all have to put our ingenuity to good use.

Eugène went to see you at Saint-Germain; you had gone out that day. I was pleased to hear that your home in Passy had been spared. I also noticed today this poor Oudinot, who also had his hour of power. What a fall! I think, Mademoiselle, that you won't remain long in Cherbourg. In any case, everyone is returning to Paris, it's impossible to live anywhere else.

Comments on art

Manet's only writing on art was the preface to a booklet accompanying his exhibition at the Alma Pavilion, at the gates of the World Fair of 1867 – and it was more of a tactical defence than an aesthetic manifesto. He was, however, a brilliant conversationalist, and a few of his comments have been gathered here.

Since 1861 Manet has been exhibiting, or trying to exhibit.

This year he has decided to show the sum total of his works to the public.

Eva Gonzalès (1870, top) and Berthe Morisot (1872–4, above).

Pinks and Clematis in a Crystal Vase (1882?). Antonin Proust remembered Manet saying, 'A painter can say everything with fruits and flowers, or with clouds only.... I would like to be like the Saint Francis of the still life.'

Manet received an honourable mention when he first exhibited at the Salon. But since then he has seen himself rejected by the jury too often not to think that, if an artist's beginning is a struggle, at least one might fight with equal weapons. That is to say one must be able also to exhibit what one has done.

Without that the artist would be all too easily shut up in a circle from which there is no exit. He would be forced either to stack his canvases or roll them up in a hayloft.

It is said that official recognition, encouragement and rewards are actually a guarantee of talent in the eyes of a certain part of the public; they are thereby forewarned in behalf of or against the accepted or rejected works. But, on the other hand, the painter is assured that it is the spontaneous impression of this same public that motivates the chilly welcome the various juries give his canvases.

In these circumstances the artist has been advised to wait.

To wait for what? Until there is no longer a jury?

He has preferred to settle the question with the public.

The artist does not say, 'Come and see faultless work,' but rather, 'Come and see sincere work.'

This sincerity gives the work a character of protest, albeit the painter merely thought of rendering his impression.

Manet has never wished to protest. It is rather against the man who did not expect it that people have protested, because there is a traditional system of teaching form, technique and appearances in painting, and because those who have been brought up according to such principles do not acknowledge any other. From that they derive their naive intolerance. Outside of their formulas nothing is valid, and they become not only critics but adversaries, and active adversaries.

To exhibit is for the artist the vital concern, the *sine qua non*; for it happens that after looking at something you become used to what was surprising or, if you wish, shocking. Little by little you understand and accept it.

Time itself imperceptibly works on paintings and softens the original harshness.

To exhibit is to find friends and allies for the struggle.

Manet has always recognized talent wherever he found it and has presumed neither to overthrow earlier painting nor to make it new. He has merely tried to be himself and not someone else. Besides, Manet has found important encouragement and has been able to see how much the judgment of men of real talent is daily becoming more favourable towards him. Therefore it is now only a question for the painter of gaining the good will of the public which has been turned into a would-be enemy.

Manet's preface to his May 1867 exhibition catalogue

We're in a pitiful state. Who was it who said that drawing was the handwriting of the figure? The truth is that art must be the writing of life. In short, at the Ecole des Beaux-Arts, one does beautiful work, but dirty business.

Manet
Comments made at Couture's studio, as recalled by Antonin Proust, 1897

On the subject of the expression 'Impressionism', which did not arise, as M. Benedite wrote, from a work of Claude Monet's exhibited under the title *Impression*, but which arose from our discussions of 1858, when he volunteered: 'An artist must be spontaneous. That is the right term. But to have spontaneity, he must be the master of his art. Experimentation never leads anywhere. You have to translate what you feel, but translate instantaneously, if you will. One speaks of people being slow on the uptake. But one never speaks of the staircase of the mind. Countless people try to climb it but never reach the top, so difficult is it to climb its steps. Invariably, one notices that what one did one day is no longer consistent with what one does the next.'

Manet, as recalled by Antonin Proust

I myself worry very little about what could have been said on art. But if I had to give an opinion, I would formulate one in this way: everything that has the soul of humanity, everything that has the soul of contemporaneity is interesting. Everything that is deprived of it is worthless.

Manet, as recalled by Antonin Proust

I came back to see him during my stay and he told me things like this: concision in art is a necessity as well as an elegance; a man who is concise makes you think, a verbose man bores you. Always move in the direction of concision. In a figure look for the highest light and the deepest shadow, the rest will come quite naturally: often it's nothing at all. And then, cultivate your memories; nature will never give you anything but hints – it's like a railing that keeps you from falling into banality. You must constantly remain the master and do as you please. No tasks! No, no tasks!...

Colour, Manet went on, is a matter of taste and sensibility. For instance, you must have something to say, otherwise good night. You are not a painter if you don't love painting more than anything else, but it is not enough to know your métier, you must also be moved. Knowledge is all very well, but for us, you see, imagining matters more.

Georges Jeanniot
'En souvenir de Manet'
La Grande Revue, 10 August 1907

Bellevue
14 Juillet 1880

Vive l'amnistie

E. Manet

Je ne vous écris
plus vous ne me
repondez jamais

Bellevue
9 Juillet

C'est un petit bonjour
en passant, j'aimerais
en recevoir un dans
les matins à l'heure
du laurier - je suis sûr

Bellevue

Décidément vous ne vous
gatez pas - ou vous
êtes bien occupée ou
vous êtes bien méchante.
cependant on n'a pas le
courage de vous en vouloir.

When he was cloistered at Bellevue during the summer of 1880, next to the hydrotherapy clinic where he was being treated for his locomotive ataxia, Manet wrote friends charming letters adorned with watercolours. Three of these melancholy missives were addressed to Isabelle Lemonnier. In the letter above, two flags celebrate the amnesty of the Communards on 14 July, with these words: 'I will no longer write to you, you never answer me.' Under the cat above right: 'This is a little hello in passing, I would like to receive post every morning.' Over the rosebud he has written: 'Either you are very busy, or you are very cruel. Still, I don't have the courage to hold it against you.'

Cordialités,
E. Manet

Olympia: scandals and triumphs

'Like a man who has fallen in the snow, Manet has made an impression on public opinion,' wrote Champfleury to Baudelaire about Olympia *at the Salon of 1865.*

1428

This cartoon by Cham appeared in *Le Charivari* on 14 May 1865. It was called 'Manet: "The Birth of the Little Slave Trader" ' and the caption read: 'M. Manet has taken the matter too literally: what a bouquet of flowers! The notices were in the name of Mother Michél and her cat [a popular French song].'

A *succès de scandale*

The clamour set off by the *Olympia* and the *Jesus Mocked* added to the previous noise made by the *Déjeuner sur l'Herbe*, gave to Manet the kind of notoriety that no other painter had had before. Cartoons of all kinds, newspapers of all types of opinion, had set about with such persistence to cover him and his works that he became universally known. Degas could say without exaggeration that Manet was as famous as Garibaldi. When he went out on the street, passers-by turned around to watch him. When he entered a public place, his arrival caused a stir, one or another singling him out as an odd creature. A young man might have been contented to be so noticed, but the public attention, in the form that it was given, soon destroyed whatever satisfaction might have been enjoyed by the man who received it.

Théodore Duret
Manet, 1906

If the canvas of the *Olympia* was not slashed and destroyed, it is only because of the precautions that were taken by the administration…. One evening, leaving the Salon, we entered the Imoda ice-cream parlour, at the top of the Rue Royale. The waiter brought the papers. 'Who asked for newspapers?' said Manet. After a long silence, we returned to his studio…. I never saw Manet more sorrowful than that day.

Antonin Proust
Edouard Manet, Souvenirs
1897

It is understandable why Manet did not want to see the newspapers, in light of what follows.

A short anthology of insults received by *Olympia* at the Salon of 1865 from the most recognized critics of the period

These terrible canvases, challenges to the mob, pranks or parodies, what can I say?... What's this yellow-bellied Odalisque, this vile model picked up who knows where, and who represents Olympia? Olympia? What Olympia? A courtesan, no doubt. No one will reproach M. Manet for idealizing mad virgins, when it's he who paints indecent ones.

Jules Claretie

Olympia can be understood from no point of view, even if you take it for what it is, a puny model stretched out on a sheet. The colour of the flesh is dirty.... The shadows are indicated by more or less large smears of blacking.... We would still forgive the ugliness, were it only truthful, carefully studied, heightened by some splendid effect of colour.... Here there is nothing, we are sorry to say, but the desire to attract attention at any price.

Théophile Gautier

I must say that the grotesque aspect of her expression is the result of two factors: first, an almost childish ignorance of the first elements of drawing, then a bent for an inconceivable vulgarity.

Ernest Chesneau

The mob, as at the Morgue, crowds around the spicy *Olympia* and the frightful *Ecce Homo* by Manet. Art sunk so low does not even deserve reproach.

Paul de Saint-Victor

Two years later, Olympia *found in Emile Zola a brilliant defender, profoundly influenced by his discussions with Manet in his studio.*

In 1865 Manet was again accepted at the Salon; he exhibited a *Christ Mocked by the Soldiers* and his masterpiece, his *Olympia*. I said masterpiece, and I will not retract the word. I maintain that this canvas is truly the painter's flesh and blood. It is all his and his alone. It will endure as the characteristic expression of his talent, as the highest mark of his power. In it I read the personality of Manet and when I analysed the artist's temperament I had before me only this canvas which sums up all the others. Here we have, as the popular jokers say, an Epinal print. Olympia, reclining on the white sheets, is a large pale spot on the black background. In this black background are the head of a negress carrying a bouquet and the famous cat which has entertained the public so much. Thus at the first glance you distinguish only two tones in the painting, two strong tones played off against each other. Moreover, details have disappeared. Look at the head of the young girl. The lips are two narrow pink lines, the eyes are reduced to a few black strokes. Now look closely at the bouquet. Some patches of pink, blue and green. Everything is simplified and if you wish to reconstruct reality you must step back a bit. Then a curious thing happens. Each object falls into its proper plane. Olympia's head projects from the background in astonishing relief, the bouquet becomes marvellously fresh and brilliant. An accurate eye and a direct hand performed this miracle. The painter

An etching and aquatint of *Olympia* (1867).

worked as nature works, in simple masses and large areas of light, and his work has the somewhat rude and austere appearance of nature itself. In addition there is a personal quality; art lives only by prejudice. And this bias is found in just that elegant austerity, that violence of transitions which I have pointed out. This is the personal accent, the particular savour of his work. Nothing is more exquisitely refined than the pale tones of the white linen on which Olympia reclines. In that juxtaposition of these various whites an immense difficulty has been overcome. The child's body itself is charmingly pallid. She is a girl of sixteen, doubtless some model whom Edouard Manet has quietly copied just as she was. And everyone exclaimed that this nude body was indecent. That's as it should be since here in the flesh is a girl whom the artist has put on canvas in her youthful, slightly tarnished nakedness. When other artists correct nature by painting Venus they lie. Manet asked himself why he should lie. Why not tell the

truth? He has introduced us to Olympia, a girl of our own times, whom we have met in the streets pulling a thin shawl of faded wool over her narrow shoulders. As usual the public took good care not to understand what the painter wanted. There are even people who have looked for a philosophical meaning in the painting. Others, less restrained, would not have been displeased to find an indecent intention.

And tell them with your voice raised, dear master, that you are not at all what they imagine, and that, for you, a picture is an opportunity for analysis. You wanted a nude, and you took Olympia, the first to come along; you wanted bright, luminous patches, and the bouquet served; you wanted black patches, and you added a black woman and a black cat. What does all this mean? You hardly know, nor do I. But I do know that you succeeded admirably in creating a painting, and a great painting, and in translating into a special language the truths of light and shade, the realities of people and things.

Emile Zola
Une nouvelle manière en peinture,
1867

Monet, *Olympia* and the museum

Seven years after Manet's death, in 1890, Monet would spend almost a year fighting to have Olympia *purchased by a group of artists and connoisseurs; he then offered the work to the State.*

Monsieur le Ministre,

In the name of a group of sub-scribers, I have the honour of offering to the State Edouard Manet's *Olympia*.

We are certain that we represent a great number of artists, writers and art-lovers, who have long recognized the important place in the history of this century held by the painter who has been prematurely lost to his art and his country....

The great majority of those who are interested in French painting agree that Edouard Manet's role was useful and decisive. Not only did he play an important individual part, he was also the representative of a great and fruitful development.

It seems impossible to us that such a work does not belong in our national collections, that the master is denied entrance where his pupils have already been admitted. In addition, we have noted with concern the incessant movement of the art market, the competition from America and the easily foreseen departure for another continent of so many works of art that are the joy and the glory of France. We wanted to retain one of Edouard Manet's most characteristic works, one where he appears in full victorious struggle, as master of his vision and of his craft.

We therefore put *Olympia* in your hands, Monsieur le Ministre. It is our desire to see it take its place in the Louvre, when the time comes, among the work of the French school. If regulations preclude its immediate entry, we believe that the Musée du Luxembourg is the obvious choice to receive *Olympia*, and to keep it until the question can be reconsidered.

Monet to Armand Fallières
Minister of Public Education
7 February 1890

From sacred horror to the wrapped gift

Olympia shocked, aroused a sacred horror, imposed herself and triumphed. She was a scandal, an idol, a public presence and a powerful skeleton in society's cupboard. Her head is empty; a black velvet string isolates it from the essence of her being.... A bestial vestal virgin consecrated to the nude absolute, she bears dreams of all the primitive barbarism and animal ritual retained and hidden in the customs and practices of urban prostitution.

Paul Valéry
Triomphe de Manet, 1932

The last impediment to utter naked-ness, with the exception of the jewel at her wrist and the mules ready to leave her feet: the neck band – hardly more than a thread – whose knot, as neat as the tie on a gift package, above the rich offering of the two breasts, forms a bow to be undone easily by pulling an end.

More than an ornament, this bauble, which perhaps for Manet was nothing more than a capricious drawing breaking up the whiteness of the nude, is for us the needless detail which sticks and which makes *Olympia* exist.

Michel Leiris
Le Ruban au cou d'Olympia, 1981

Visits to the studio

Manet worked in seven studios, the most important being on the Rue Guyot, behind the Parc Monceau. Then he moved into a succession of studios in the new Europe quarter, near the Saint-Lazare railway station. From 1870 to 1878, he was on the Rue de Saint-Pétersbourg (numbers 51 and 4), and finally in 1878 he moved to the Rue d'Amsterdam (number 70, then 77), where he remained until his death in 1883.

Zola posing in the studio

I recall those long hours of sitting. In the numbness that overtakes motionless limbs, in the fatigue of gazing open-eyed in full light, the same thoughts would always drift through my mind, with a soft, deep murmur. The nonsense abroad in the streets, the lies of some and the inanities of others, all that human noise which flows as worthless as foul water, was far, far away.... At times, in the half-sleep of posing, I would watch the artist, standing before the canvas, with his face tense and a clear eye, absorbed in his task. He had forgotten me, he didn't know I was there, he was copying me as he would have copied any human animal, with an attention, an artistic awareness, the like of which I have never seen.... All about me, on the walls of the studio, were hung those characteristically powerful canvases the public has not cared to understand.

Emile Zola
'Mon salon', 23 May 1868

Manet in his studio

At the entrance the artist came towards us, smiling affably and offering his hand in friendly fashion. We went into the hall, a large room panelled in dark antique oak with a ceiling of beams alternating with dark-coloured coffers. A clear, soft, unvarying light enters through the windows overlooking the Place de l'Europe. The railway passes close by, giving off plumes of white smoke which swirl in the air. The ground, continually shaken, trembles underfoot and shudders like the deck

Detail from Henri Fantin-Latour's *A Studio in the Batignolles* (1870).

of a ship at sea. In the distance, the view extends down the Rue de Rome, with its attractive ground-floor gardens and imposing houses. Then, on the heights of the Boulevard des Batignolles a sombre dark hollow: it is the tunnel, an obscure and mysterious orifice devouring the trains which plunge under its vault with a sharp whistle.

On the walls were some of the painter's works. First of

Drawing by Manet of visitors to his studio in 1876.

all the famous *Déjeuner sur l'Herbe*, rejected by the jury which stupidly did not understand that this is not a naked woman, but a woman undressed, which is quite different. Then the paintings exhibited on other occasions: *The Music Lesson, The Balcony, Olympia* with her negress and her strange black cat which is certainly a close relative of Hoffmann's famous Mürr.... Then a *Seascape*, the sketch of two women seated in the middle of a field, surrounded by a village, a portrait of a woman and an exquisite *Punch*, pluckily seated.

But we now come to the new. There is something altogether remarkable on this easel at the foot of the oak staircase which leads up to the tribunal, where one once judged the moves when this magnificent atelier was a fencing school....

This canvas, which was destined for [the celebrated opera singer Jean-Baptiste] Faure, depicted the corridor of the Opéra the night of a masked ball. That is the very work. Between the massive pillars of the amphitheatre wall, where the swells stand *en espalier*, and the lobby entrances separated by the legendary red velvet panels, there ebbs and flows a tide of black cloth on which floats an occasional Pierrette or *débardeuse* ['stevedorette'].…

Groups form in diverse attitudes. An impudent Gavroche, a blossom sprung from two gutter cobbles and – mystery of mysteries – lovely as a Grecian statue, in a state of undress to challenge the Sixth Commandment, pantalooned in a red velvet rag no bigger than a man's hand, with plenty of buttons to be sure, and with cap set at forty-five degrees on her powdered tangle of hair, leads a troupe of white-tied revellers. There they all are, alight with Corton and truffles, with moist lip and sensual eye, with gold chains across their vests and rings set with gems on their fingers. Hats tilted back with an air of conquest: they are rich, that is clear…and they have come to enjoy themselves.

Perhaps there is not all this in the painting; perhaps there is more besides? At any rate, it is a work of high merit, alive, thoughtful and admirably rendered. We shall see, at the next Salon, whether the public is of my opinion.

Fervacques
Le Figaro, 27 December 1873

This portrait of Eva Gonzalès was probably painted in Manet's studio, where she was both a model and student.

The ateliers of 1875–83

I must have been thirteen or fourteen years old when I was taken to see Manet's studio, his first studio on the Rue de Saint-Pétersbourg, and which overlooked the middle of the Europe bridge. It was a sitting room with brown and gilded panelling, a dentist's waiting room. On the wall, a canvas depicting M. and Mme Astruc, playing the mandolin. We were invited to see a portrait of Desboutin.

Was it this time, or later, that I saw on the easel *The Laundry*, then altogether fresh, and dazzling in its light, of a blue so bright and so cheerful that it made one want to sing?…

How could Manet work in this room filled with sunlight? Is this where he completed *The Laundry*, *The Railway*, *Argenteuil*? 'The outdoor school' was often held indoors.…

The second studio on the Rue de Saint-Pétersbourg was the headquarters of important political meetings. During the day it received northern light, it was common and cold, in the rear of a courtyard where a number of artists lived.… In front of Manet's door, there were a few flowerpots and green tubs filled with laurel, just as on the terraces of the cafés during that period. A great deal of promiscuity prevailed among the neighbours, but after the studio session, everyone met at Manet's.

I still see him leaning on his cane filled with a leaden tip, trying to maintain his balance on his rubber heels. He prided himself on his handsome feet, dressed in 'English boots'; he often wore a pleated and belted Norfolk jacket, like an English sportsman. He hated the dauber's style. In a corner of the entryway, flopped on

Surrounding Manet in Fantin-Latour's celebrated *A Studio in the Batignolles*, from left to right, are the German painter Scholderer, then Renoir, Astruc, Zola, the musician Edmond Maitre, Bazille and finally Monet.

the red sofa, were Albert Wolff, Aurélien Scholl, boulevardiers and demimondaines gathered around him....

The studio of 77 Rue de Saint-Pétersbourg [in fact, Rue d'Amsterdam] was in no way that of the man who represented a master whose name was to dominate the end of the 19th century and the beginning of the 20th. A shed for forgotten canvases, most of them rolled up, it resembled those of my comrades who seemed to work, but who in fact received women. A few rare pieces of furniture, picked up here and there, a restaurant buffet, where the girl with the blue bodice leaned her hands in *Bar at the Folies-Bergère*; a few vases of flowers, litre bottles, flasks of liqueurs, a few bottles of champagne on the table where the two lovers sat for *At Père Lathuille's Restaurant*; the footed mirror in *Nana*, a zinc tub. On the easels, a few pastels, of George Moore and Méry Laurent, the friend of Henry Duprey and of Mallarmé, Manet's daily visitor, at the hour when one came to talk and laugh. On the chairs, a silk corsage, a hat, which after the model's departure, Manet copies with diligence so as 'to make it stay on the head'. There is nothing more difficult to draw than a top hat, Manet used to say....

Jacques-Emile Blanche
in *Propos de peinture, de David à Degas*, 1919

The triumph of Manet

Even though the established art critics and journalists were always relatively severe to the painter, Manet had the good fortune to attract, both in the course of his life and after his death, other remarkable writers: Charles Baudelaire, Emile Zola, Stéphane Mallarmé, then Paul Valéry, André Malraux and Georges Bataille.

Baudelaire, his first defender

Baudelaire no longer wrote about the Salons by the time Manet began to show his work. But he supported him in other ways, as can be seen in these excerpts from his letters.

I want to thank you for the pleasure you have given me in coming to the defence of my friend Edouard Manet, and in dealing him a little bit of justice. However, there are a few small points to straighten out in the opinions that you have published.

Manet, whom people think wild and insane, is simply a very straightforward, unaffected person, as reasonable as he can be but unfortunately touched by romanticism at birth.

The word 'imitation' is unfair. Manet has never seen a Goya; Manet has never seen a Greco; Manet has never seen the Pourtalès Collection. This seems unbelievable to you, but it's true.

I have myself admired, in amazement, these mysterious coincidences.

At the time when we used to enjoy that wonderful Spanish museum, which the stupid French Republic in its excessive respect for private property gave back to the House of Orléans, Manet was a youngster serving in the navy. People have told him so much about his imitations of Goya that he is now trying to see some Goyas.

It is true that he has seen Velázquez, I know not where....

Do not be annoyed, but keep in some corner of your mind a kind thought for me. Every time you try to do a good deed for Manet, I shall thank you...

Baudelaire to Théophile Thoré
c. 20 June 1864

Manet's talent is strong and will endure. But his character is weak. He seems to me to be prostrated and stunned by the blow. What strikes me also is the joy of all those imbeciles who think he has lost.

Baudelaire to Champfleury
25 May 1865

Brilliant faculties

When you see Manet, tell him this: that torment – whether it be great or small – that mockery, that insults, that injustice are excellent things, and that he should be ungrateful were he not thankful for injustice. I well know he will have some difficulty understanding my theory; painters always want immediate success. But really, Manet has such brilliant and facile ability that it would be unfortunate if he became discouraged. He will never be able to fill completely the gaps in his temperament. But he has a *temperament*, that's the important thing. And he does not seem to suspect that the greater the injustice, the better the situation – on condition that he does not lose his head. (You will know how to say this lightly, and without hurting him.)

Baudelaire to Mme Paul Meurice
24 May 1865

Valéry, Manet and Baudelaire

Even if he never met Manet, Paul Valéry heard a great deal about him. The poet had in fact married the niece of Berthe Morisot-Manet and lived in the family house surrounded by the work of her aunt and her brother-in-law, Manet. A great admirer of both the painter and Baudelaire, he sensed the affinity between the two men.

Manet, still seduced by the exotically picturesque, while given over to the

A n etching and aquatint of Baudelaire (1867–8).

matador, the guitar and the mantilla, was already half conquered by objects closer to him, as well as by models in the street. This situation represented for Baudelaire the very problem he himself had; that is, the critical state of an artist who is prey to rival temptations, and, in addition to which, was capable of expressing himself admirably in several ways.

You only need to leaf through the slender collection of *Les Fleurs du mal*, to observe the concentrated diversity of theme in these poems, to associate them with the diversity of subjects in the body of Manet's work, and to conclude fairly easily that the poet and the painter shared similar concerns.

A man who wrote *Bénédiction, Tableaux parisiens*, the *Bijoux* and the *Vin des chiffonniers* and the man who in turn painted *Christ with the Angels* and *Olympia, Lola* and *The Absinthe Drinker* are not without some profound resemblance.

A few observations allow one to strengthen this relationship. Descended from that old Parisian bourgeoisie, both of them showed that same rare refined elegance in their taste and their singular will for rigour in execution.

Moreover, they equally repulse those effects that do not emanate from a clear conscience and from the possession of their faculties in their crafts; it is in this that consists the *purity* in the areas of painting and poetry. They wanted nothing to do with speculation over 'sentiment' nor the introduction of 'ideas' without knowledgeably and subtly mastering 'sensation'. In short, they pursued and reunited with the ultimate objective of their art, enchantment, a term that I use here with all its force.

Paul Valéry
Triomphe de Manet
1932

Zola

Emile Zola was the most talented and the greatest journalistic supporter throughout Manet's career, notably in 1866 and 1867, when he discussed the Olympia. *But in the 1870s, the 'Impressionist' direction adopted by the painter disappointed him. Still, he was happy that Manet never read his novel* L'Oeuvre, *published in 1886, in which the failed painter is a mingling of Manet and Cézanne.*

He sometimes gets off course

He has been unable to work out his own methods; he remains an excitable student, seeing very accurately what takes place in nature, but not sure that he can definitively and fully transmit his impressions. Therefore when he starts out on his own path,

you are not sure how he will reach the end of it or whether he will reach it at all. He works at random. When one of his paintings succeeds, then it is indeed extraordinary, absolutely truthful and unusually skilful. But sometimes he makes mistakes, and then his paintings are uneven and incomplete. In short, during the past fifteen years there has not appeared another more individual artist. If the technical side of the matter were equal to the accuracy of his impressions, he would be a great painter of the second half of the 19th century.

Emile Zola
in *Viestnik Europi*
Saint Petersburg, June 1879

'The eye, a hand'

That a tragic fate – aside from the fact that he was cheated of glory by Death, the universal conspirator – that a harsh and hostile destiny should have denied a man pleasure and grace disturbs me: not the vilification of the latest – and instinctive – reinventor of our great pictorial tradition, nor the fact of a merely posthumous gratitude. Yet amid the disappointments and vexations, behold the virile naiveté of a faun in putty-coloured greatcoat, his thinning blond hair and beard going smartly grey. To all appearances a café wit, and elegant; yet in the studio, a demiurge flinging himself upon the canvas in frenzy, as if he had never painted before – what was once a precocious talent for unsettling us, here pursued with happy strokes of inspiration and sudden mitigations: a lesson to my daily attendance, a lesson that one must risk oneself entire and anew each time, a total virtuality even while remaining, quite deliberately,

Manet's portrait of Edgar Allan Poe and the poster for 'The Raven', which Mallarmé translated.

oneself. How fervently he used to say, in those days, 'the eye, a hand' – it all comes back to me now.

Manet's eye – the eye of generations of city-bred childhoods, when brought to bear, quite new, virginal and abstract, on an object, on persons, sustained to the last the immediate freshness of the encounter; gripped in the talons of a glancing laugh, teasingly exorcising the exasperations of what would turn out to be the twentieth sitting. Manet's hand – its pressure registered as distinct and ready – expressed how mysteriously the limpidity of looking penetrated, in order to order, lively and laved, profound, intense or obsessed by certain black contours, the masterpiece, new and French.

Stéphane Mallarmé
'Manet'
Divigations, 1896

An art historian's point of view

Manet hardly considered himself a revolutionary and probably did not even want to be one. There was none of the provocative element in him which had always made Courbet the center of discussions; his independence was not an attitude chosen to force attention, it was the natural condition in which he lived and worked. Little did he expect that this independence might be considered a challenge by others and that he would have to fight in order to maintain his right to be himself. But he was ready to fight. He had been and still was of the opinion that the Salon was the natural place for an artist to introduce himself, yet this did not mean that he accepted the jury's decision. Somehow he hoped, as doubtless most of the others did, that the public would be on his side and prove the jury wrong. There even seemed to be a vague possibility that a success of the Salon des Refusés might lead to the complete suppression of the jury, for which the realists and their friends had already fought for years....

Zacharie Astruc expressed himself more specifically about the rejected artists. For the duration of the exhibition he founded a daily paper, *Le Salon de 1863*, in which he had the courage to write: 'Manet! One of the greatest artistic characters of the time! I would not say that he carries off the laurels in this Salon…but he is its brilliance, inspiration, powerful flavor, surprise. Manet's talent has a decisive side that startles; something trenchant, sober, and energetic, that reflects his nature, which is both reserved and exalted, and above all sensitive to intense impressions.'

Of the three paintings exhibited by Manet, two derived their colour accents from picturesque Spanish costumes; one was a portrait of his brother, *Young Man in the Costume of a Majo*; the other, *Mlle V… in the Costume of an Espada*, had been posed for by his favorite model, Victorine Meurent. The third canvas, listed under the title *Le Bain*, was later to be called *Le Déjeuner sur l'Herbe*. It was this last picture that immediately attracted all visitors, the more so because the Emperor had pronounced it 'immodest'. Mr Hamerton [an English art critic] agreed with the monarch when he wrote: 'I ought not to omit a remarkable picture of the realist school, a translation of a thought of Giorgione into modern French. Giorgione had conceived the happy idea of a *fête champêtre* in which, although the gentlemen were dressed,

the ladies were not, but the doubtful morality of the picture is pardoned for the sake of its fine colour.… Now some wretched Frenchman has translated this into modern French realism, on a much larger scale, and with the horrible modern French costume instead of the graceful Venetian one. Yes, there they are, under the trees, the principal lady, entirely undressed…another female in a chemise coming out of a little stream that runs hard by, and two Frenchmen in wide-awakes sitting on the very green grass with a stupid look of bliss. There are other pictures of the same class, which lead to the inference that the nude, when painted by vulgar men, is inevitably indecent.'

As a matter of fact, the central group of Manet's *Déjeuner sur l'Herbe*, though superficially related to Giorgione, had been adapted from an engraving after Raphael. Indeed a curious lack of imagination repeatedly led Manet to 'borrow' subjects from other artists. Many of his works, if not based directly on old masters, were at least inspired by remembrance (Manet had travelled extensively), by reproductions, prints, etc. Although Manet himself rarely made any allusions to his sources, he often used them with so little disguise that it would have been easy to identify them had anybody cared to do so. But in Manet's case the whole question seemed of little importance, since what mattered was not the subject but the way in which he treated it. He found in works of the past only compositional elements; he never copied, because only his inspiration, not his talent, needed an occasional guide. As Degas later explained it: 'Manet drew inspiration from everywhere, from Monet, Pissarro, even from me. But with what marvelous handling of the brush did he not make something new of it! He had no initiative… and did not do anything without thinking of Velázquez and Hals. When he painted a fingernail, he would remember that Hals never let the nails extend beyond the fingers themselves, and proceeded likewise. He felt only one ambition, to become famous and to earn money. I told him to be satisfied with being appreciated by an elite; one who works with so much refinement cannot expect to be understood by the masses.' Yet the irony of fate caused Manet to be attacked for the 'vulgarity' of his inspiration, even in cases where he had derived his themes from the classic masters.

It may be doubted whether Manet's painting would have provoked such criticism had it not been painted in broad contrasts and frank oppositions, with a tendency to simplification. His 'vulgarity', in the eyes of the public, lay probably even more in his execution than in his subject matter. It was his renunciation of the customary slick brushwork, his fashion of summarily

Manet's illustration for 'The Raven'.

indicating background details and of obtaining forms without the help of lines, by opposing colours or by sketching his contours, if necessary, with decisive brushstrokes in colour (which helped to model volumes instead of limiting them), that were responsible for the almost universal disapproval he met.…

Compared with the prestige of ridicule obtained by Manet and Whistler, most of the other exhibitors at the Salon des Refusés fared rather well with the public and the reviewers. Pissarro even drew a few favorable lines from a renowned critic, who advised him, nevertheless, to be careful not to imitate Corot. Among the young painters outside the Academy, Manet's stature grew immensely through this exhibition so as to make him appear the leader of the new generation (Cézanne, Bazille, Zola were among those deeply impressed), and when Whistler and Fantin took a recent British acquaintance, the nineteen-year-old Swinburne, to the painter's studio, this visit became a highlight of the latter's trip to Paris. 'He [Manet] doubtless does not remember it,' the poet wrote many years later to Mallarmé, 'but for me, then very young and completely unknown…you may well believe it is a memory which will not easily be forgotten.'

John Rewald
The History of Impressionism, 1946

The representation of the world

It was said that Manet didn't know how to paint a centimetre of skin, and that the *Olympia* was drawn in steel wire; one forgot only that before wanting to 'draw' *Olympia* or paint her skin, he first wanted to make paintings.…

The painting, whose background was a hole, became a surface, and this surface became not only its own design, but its only design. The most imperious sketches of Delacroix were still dramatizations; what Manet undertook in certain canvases was the representation of the world. For if it already happened that his brushwork took on this autonomy which ultimately would be vindicated, it was only in the service of a passion of which painting was only the means.… The objective of that keenness of vision is only a means, it is the transformation of things into a autonomous plastic universe, coherent and distinctive.…

What Manet brought, not in any way superior, but in being irreducibly different, was the green of the *Balcony*, the pink splotch of the gown in the *Olympia*, the patch of raspberry behind the black bodice of *Bar at the Folies-Bergère*.… It was tradition brought back to the pleasure of painting.

André Malraux,
*Psychologie de l'art –
Le Musée imaginaire*, 1947

Supreme indifference

Manet's sober elegance, bared elegance, quickly attained a rectitude, not only in its indifference, but in the active sureness of how it knew to show indifference. The indifference of Manet is indifference supreme, which, while scandalizing, doesn't deign to know that it carries scandal within it.…

For often, indifference is a force; because a force, otherwise constrained, is liberated within indifference. Here Manet's joy in painting, which he took to the level of a passion, mixed with that divine indifference which opposed the mythological world where Raphael and Titian took delight. Here was the affirmation of a sober power which went along with a sober rejoicing in destruction. Manet attained the silence of freedom that his virtuosity gave him: at the same time it was the silence of rigorous destruction. *Olympia* was the culmination of that elegance in that in the play of those rare colours there was the same intensity of the negation of an accepted world.…

We can discover in others as in Manet the transition in painting, of a language that tells, that is of an 'imagined or real spectacle'.… We cannot not see a glimmer appear in the painting of Chardin or of Delacroix, of Courbet or of Turner. Perhaps a little bit everywhere in painting…

But it is expressly to Manet that we first owe the birth of this painting with no other meaning than the art of painting which is 'modern painting'.

Georges Bataille
Naissance de la peinture moderne, 1955

Champfleury asked Manet to make a poster for his work *Les Chats* (1868).

J. ROTHSCHILD, ÉDITEUR, 43, RUE St-ANDRÉ-DES-ARTS, PARIS

CHAMPFLEURY

LES CHATS

HISTOIRE – MŒURS – ANECDOTES

ILLUSTRÉ
PAR

E. Delacroix

Breughel

Viollet-le-Duc

ILLUSTRÉ
PAR

Ed. Manet

Ok'Sai

Mind, Ribot

UN VOLUME ORNÉ DE NOMBREUSES GRAVURES

PRIX : **5** FRANCS

Paris. — Typ. Goutet, rue du Jardinet, 1.

A few comments from painters

Manet was a painter loved by other painters, first by his contemporaries Fantin-Latour and Degas, and then by all the young artists who saw in him a model of freedom and modernity, from Monet and Cézanne to Matisse and Picasso. Picasso reinterpreted Le Déjeuner sur l'Herbe *from 1959 to 1962 in a series of works where he showed himself to be both an iconoclast and an admirer.*

PORTRAIT DU TINTORET.

J'autorise M. Manet à reproduire ma binette, à condition qu'il ne la montrera à personne.

TINTORET.

Cézanne

What made Manet a real forerunner was that he brought a simple formula to a period when officially accepted art was nothing but bombast and convention.

Recalled by Ambroise Vollard, 1924

Degas

Courbet said he's never seen any angels and so could not know if they have backsides, and furthermore, given their size, it is unlikely that the wings that Manet put on them could support them. But I don't give a damn about all that, because there is real drawing in this *Christ with the Angels!* And the transparent quality of the paint! Oh! the pig!

ME – Ingres never worked outdoors, but didn't Manet work outdoors?

DEGAS (annoyed) – Don't say the word 'outdoors' in front of me anymore. Poor Manet! Having painted the *Maximilian*, the *Christ with the Angels*, and all that he did until 1875, he then let go of his magnificent 'eye' to paint *The Laundry!*…

Recalled by Ambroise Vollard, 1924

Pissarro

Manet was greater than us; he was able to make light out of black.

Recalled by Ambroise Vollard, 1924

Signac

What a painter! He has everything, an intelligent mind, an impeccable eye, and what a hand!

From *Journal*, in *La Gazette des Beaux-Arts*, 1949

The caption under this caricature by Randon reads: 'I authorize M. Manet to reproduce my face, on the condition that he shows it to no one. Tintoretto.'

Portraits of Manet by Degas (1866–8) and Monet by Manet (1879–80, below).

Gauguin

He once told me, having seen a work of mine (when I was just beginning), that it was very good; I retorted out of respect for his mastery: 'I am only an amateur.' At the time I was working as a stockbroker and was studying art only at night and on holidays.

'No,' said Manet.... 'The only amateurs are those who do bad painting.' That was music to my ears.

Avant et Après, 1923

Jacques-Emile Blanche

There aren't two paintings in his entire body of work that weren't inspired by another painting, antique or modern.... There was no one who 'plagiarized' more and no one who was more original.... Always and everywhere, the *touch* was Manet's, his paint was unique; his awkwardness, his simultaneous precision and resolution were his alone. It is well done even in the

apparent carelessness. There is a fullness in the simplified and awkward drawing, there is distortion in the feeling of grandeur. His flat modelling eliminates certain planes, gives a unique quality to his still life, to objects. Do you remember the *Ham* on the silver platter, the *Bunch of Asparagus.* No one ever painted like that before him....

A painter of great craftsmanship can be inspired, must be inspired by what he loves and re-create it in his own way. There are artists devoid of inventiveness and personality, whose style suggests no resemblance to any other style, and who are nonetheless insipid and of no interest. Originality resides less in the conception than in the execution. The means are everything in painting.

Propos de peintre, de David à Degas, 1919

Matisse

The Orientals used black as a colour, notably the Japanese in their prints. Nearer home, in a painting by Manet (*The Luncheon*) I recall that the black velvet jacket of the young man in a straw hat is a bold and luminous black....

B ertall's 1869 cartoon of *The Luncheon*
and Picasso's 1962 drawing inspired by
Le Déjeuner sur l'Herbe.

He was the first *to act by reflex*,
thus simplifying the painter's métier....
Manet was as direct as one could be....

A great painter is one who finds
lasting personal signs for the expression
of his vision. Manet found his.

L'Intransigeant
25 January 1932

Picasso

'When I see *Le Déjeuner sur l'Herbe*,
I say to myself: sorrows are for later.'
Said in 1932, cited in
Bonjour M. Manet, 1983

One summer day at [Picasso's home
he] told us a major piece of news: *Lola
of Valencia* had just arrived in Nice.

If it had to do with a Lola in the flesh,
an eminent personality, a Moon-man
who had just landed on the airfield, of
Sabartès or even of the children, Picasso
would have spoken no differently.

Lola of Valencia had arrived in Nice
with a few other canvases from the
same period, for an exhibition in the
city's museum....

We only spoke of *Lola of Valencia*,
the beautiful, the magnificent. Picasso
and Pignon were in the studio.
Indeed, only Manet existed. They
went through all of his canvases.
They spoke about them for an hour.

They leafed through a book where there were Manets, saying many things while raving. Only Cézanne and Van Gogh left the arena in triumph. All the rest is crap....
And what a marvellous canvas.

Cited by H. Parmelin
Picasso sur la Plage, 1959

FURTHER READING

MONOGRAPHS AND GENERAL WORKS

Bataille, Georges, *Manet*, trans. Austryn Wainhouse and James Emmons, 1983

Bazire, Edmond, *Manet*, 1884

Blanche, Jacques-Emile, *Manet*, trans. F. C. de Sumichrast, 1924

Cachin, Françoise, *Manet*, trans. Emily Read, 1991

Distel, Anne, *Les Collectionneurs des Impressionnistes*, 1989

Duret, Théodore, *Histoire d'Edouard Manet et de son oeuvre*, 1906

—, *Manet*, trans. by J. E. Crawford Flitch, 1937

Gordon, Robert, and Andrew Forge, *The Last Flower Paintings of Manet*, trans. Richard Howard, 1986

Hamilton, George Heard, *Manet and his Critics*, 1954

Hanson, Anne Coffin, *Manet and the Modern Tradition*, 1979

Hofmann, Werner, *Nana: Mythos und Wirklichkeit*, 1973

Mallarmé, Stéphane, 'The Impressionists and Edouard Manet', *Art Monthly Review*, 30 September 1876

Moore, George, *Confessions of a Young Man*, 1972

Moreau-Nélaton, Adolphe Etienne Auguste, *Manet raconté par lui-même*, 1926

Proust, Antonin, 'Edouard Manet, Souvenirs', *La Revue blanche*, February–May 1897 (revised in *L'Echoppe*, 1988)

Reff, Theodore, *Manet: Olympia*, 1976

Rewald, John, *The History of Impressionism*, 1973

Schneider, Pierre, *The World of Manet 1832–1883*, 1968

Tabarant, Adolphe, *Manet et ses oeuvres*, 1947

Vollard, Ambroise, *En ecoutant parler Cézanne, Degas, Renoir*, 1938

Wilson-Bareau, Juliet, *Manet by Himself*, 1991

Zola, Emile, 'Une Nouvelle Manière en peinture, Edouard Manet', *Revue du XIXeme Siècle*, 1 January 1867, and *E. Manet, Etude biographique et critique*, 1867

CATALOGUES OF WORKS AND EXHIBITIONS

Cachin, Françoise, and Charles S. Moffett in collaboration with Michel Melot, *Manet 1832–1883*, 1983

Guérin, Marcel, *L'Oeuvre Gravé de Manet*, 1944

Hanson, Anne Coffin, *Edouard Manet 1832–1883*, 1966

Orienti, Sandra, *The Complete Paintings of Manet*, 1985

Rouart, Denis, and Daniel Wildenstein, *Edouard Manet, Catalogue raisonné*, 1975

Reff, Theodore, *Manet and Modern Paris*, 1982

Tabarant, Adolphe, *Manet: Histoire catalographique*, 1931

Valéry, Paul, 'Triomphe de Manet', in *Manet*, 1932

Wilson, Michael, *Manet at Work*, 1983

LIST OF MUSEUMS

Where can you see Manet's greatest works? While most belong to a few select institutions (in New York, London, Paris, Chicago and Philadelphia), others are scattered in museums around the world.

Argentina
BUENOS EIRES
Museo Nacional de Bellas Artes: *The Surprised Nymph*

Belgium
TOURNAI
Musée des Beaux-Arts: *Argentueil*, *At Père Lathuille's Restaurant*

Brazil
SÃO PAULO
Museu de Arte Moderna: *Bathers in the Seine*, *The Artist*

Britain
GLASGOW, SCOTLAND
The Art Gallery and Museum: *Ham*
LONDON
Courtauld Institute Galleries: *A Bar at the Folies-Bergère*
National Gallery: *Music in the Tuileries Gardens*, *The Corner in a Café-Concert*, *Eva Gonzalès*, three parts of *The Execution of Maximilian*

France
AVIGNON
Musée Calvet: *Guitar and Hat*
DIJON
Musée des Beaux-Arts: *Méry Laurent in the Black Hat*
LE HAVRE
Musée du Havre: *Boats at Sea, Sunset*
NANCY
Musée des Beaux-Arts: *Autumn*
PARIS

Musée d'Orsay: *Portrait of M. and Mme Auguste Manet, Lola of Valencia, Le Déjeuner sur l'Herbe, Olympia, Peonies in a Vase on a Stand, Branch of White Peonies with Pruning Shears, Peony Stems and Pruning Shears, Fruit on a Table, Bullfight, The Fifer, Reading, Portrait of Emile Zola, Mme Manet at the Piano, The Balcony, Moonlight over Boulogne Harbour, The Blonde with Bare Breasts, On the Beach, Lady with the Fans/Portrait of Nina de Callias, Portrait of Stéphane Mallarmé, Girl Serving Beer, Portrait of Clemenceau, Asparagus, Pinks and Clematis in a Crystal Vase*

Musée du Petit Palais: *Portrait of Théodore Duret*

Germany
BERLIN
Staatliche Museen: *The House at Rueil, In the Conservatory*
BREMEN
Kunsthalle: *Portrait of Zacharie Astruc*
COLOGNE
Wallraf-Richartz-Museum: *Bunch of Asparagus*
ESSEN
Folkwang Museum: *Faure in the Role of Hamlet*
FRANKFURT
Städelsches Kunstinstitut: *Croquet Party in Paris*
HAMBURG
Kunsthalle: *Nana, Portrait of M. Henri Rochefort*
MANNHEIM
Städtische Kunsthalle: *The Execution of Maximilian*
MUNICH
Neue Pinakothek: *Claude Monet in his Studio, The Luncheon*

Hungary
BUDAPEST
Szépművészeti Múzeum: *Baudelaire's Mistress, Reclining*

Norway
OSLO
Nasjonalgalleriet: *L'Exposition Universelle*

Portugal
LISBON
Museu Calouste Gulbenkian: *Soap Bubbles, Child with Cherries*

Switzerland
WINTERTHUR
Oskar Reinhart collection: *At the Café*
ZURICH
Fondation Bührle: *The Port of Bordeaux, Suicide, Young Woman in Oriental Costume*

United States
CALIFORNIA
MALIBU

J. Paul Getty Museum: *The Rue Mosnier with Flags*
SAN FRANCISCO
Palace of the Legion of Honor: *The Milliner*
CONNECTICUT
FARMINGTON
Hillstead: *The Guitar-Player, La Posada*
NEW HAVEN
Yale University Art Gallery: *Young Woman Reclining in Spanish Costume*
DISTRICT OF COLUMBIA
WASHINGTON
National Gallery of Art: *Masked Ball at the Opéra, The Plum, The Railroad, The Dead Man, The Old Musician, Still Life with Melon and Peaches*
Phillips Collection: *The Spanish Ballet*
ILLINOIS
CHICAGO
Art Institute: *Bullfight, Races at Longchamp, Still Life with Fish, Jesus Mocked by the Soldiers, Steamboat, Seascape, The Philosopher, Reader at the Brasserie*
MARYLAND
BALTIMORE
Walters Art Gallery: *Café-Concert*
MASSACHUSETTS
BOSTON
Museum of Fine Arts: *The Street Singer, The Music Lesson, Portrait of Victorine Meurent*
CAMBRIDGE
Fogg Art Museum: *Skating*
NEW YORK
NEW YORK
The Metropolitan Museum of Art: *Boating, The Burial, The Monet Family in the Garden, Mlle V... in the Costume of an Espada, Young Man in the Costume of a Majo, Boy with a Sword, Fishing, Woman with a Parrot, The Spanish Singer, The Dead Christ with Angels, Portrait of George Moore, Matador Saluting*
Solomon R. Guggenheim Museum: *Before the Mirror*
OHIO
TOLEDO
Museum of Art: *Portrait of M. Antonin Proust*
PENNSYLVANIA
MERION
Barnes Foundation: *Caulking the Boat, The Laundry*
PHILADELPHIA
Philadelphia Museum of Art: *Battle of the Kearsarge and the Alabama, The Good Glass of Beer, The Steamer's Departure from Folkestone, Boats at Sea, Portrait of Emilie Ambre as Carmen*
RHODE ISLAND
PROVIDENCE
Museum of Art, Rhode Island School of Design: *Repose: Portrait of Berthe Morisot*
VERMONT
Shelburne
Shelburne Museum: *The Grand Canal, Venice (Blue Venice)*

LIST OF ILLUSTRATIONS

CHAPTER 5

The Parisian Woman, a lithograph of Nina de Callias.

Two of Manet's drawings: *Woman Standing on the Beach* and *Cats* (opposite).

INDEX

T*he Bear Trainer* (1862). Brush and brown wash over pencil.

ACKNOWLEDGMENTS

The publishers would like to thank Mme Montalant of the Galerie Hopkins-Thomas and M. Yves Rouart for their help in the creation of this book.

PHOTO CREDITS

AKG 27ar, 28a, 41l, 110l, 110r, 110–1. All rights reserved 12–3, 161l. Archives Albert Skira 57. Archives Durand-Ruel, Paris 118. Archives Roger-Viollet, Paris 13b. Artephot/Artothek, Paris 86-7. Artephot/Bridgeman, Paris 116r, 117l, 121. Artephot/Held, Paris 75a, 75b, 76a, 94a, 108a, 122r, 128. Artephot/Oroñoz, Paris 84. Artephot/Roland, Paris 21b. The Art Institute of Chicago 76–7, 82b. Artothek, Peissenberg 72a. Atelier Jean-Loup Charmet, Paris 15, 56–7, 76b, 86b, 89b. The Barnes Foundation, Merion, Pennsylvania 80–1, 104. Bibliothèque d'Art et d'Archéologie, Paris 18b, 38–9, 56a, 64a, 103, 117r, 129, 144, 161r. Bibliothèque Nationale, Paris 12, 19r, 20b, 21a, 25, 27al, 27b, 32, 35br, 35bc, 39a, 40l, 47, 48, 49, 59, 60–1, 68r, 77, 82a, 83, 87b, 89a, 91, 92a, 94–5, 98, 100, 105, 122l, 132, 137l, 137r, 138–9, 140a, 140b, 146, 153, 155l, 155r, 157, 159, 160, 162, 169, 173. Caisse Nationale des Monuments Historiques et des Sites, Paris 34bl, 34br, 35l, 107. Collection Sirot/Angel, Paris 18c, 23a, 28l, 28br, 68l, 85, 86a, 87a, 116l, 124a, 130, 135. Courtauld Institute Galleries, London 124b, 125, 126. Fogg Art Museum, Cambridge, Massachusetts 93a, 120. Galerie Hopkins-Thomas 72br. Giraudon 23b, 26, 56b, 90, 93b, 94c, 101, 123. J. Paul Getty Museum, Malibu 96–7, 97. Kunsthalle Bremen 71. Metropolitan Museum of Art, New York 3, 6, 31, 40r, 44–5, 50, 51, 63, 70r, 95, 96b, 109, 122–3. Musée Boymans, Van Beuningen, Rotterdam 41r. Musée des Beaux-Arts, Dijon 14, 115l, 115ar, 115b. Musée Marmottan, Paris 16–7. Museo Nacional des Bellas Artes, Buenos Aires 37l, 37r. Museum of Art, Philadelphia 78–9, 88, 99, 112l. Museum of Fine Arts, Boston 1, 2, 42b, 42–3, 43b, 44, 84–5. National Gallery of Art, Washington, D. C. front cover, 7, 42ar, 64–5a, 102–3, 106, 111. National Gallery, London 24, 34–5, 118–9, 150. Photothèque des Musées de la Ville de Paris 14–5, 32–3. Réunion des Musées Nationaux, Paris spine, back cover, 4, 5, 9, 10, 11, 13a, 18a, 19l, 20a, 22, 22–3, 29, 30, 33, 36al, 36ar, 36c, 36b, 38, 42al, 43a, 46, 48–9, 52–3, 54–5, 58–9, 61, 62, 64c, 64–5b, 66, 67, 69l, 69r, 70l, 72bl, 73l, 73r, 74, 92b, 96l, 96r, 100–1, 104–5, 108b, 112r, 113l, 113r, 114a, 114l, 114–5, 127, 136, 141, 143, 148, 149, 151, 162–3, 170, 171

TEXT CREDITS

Grateful acknowledgment is made for use of material from the following: (pp. 149–50: Fervacques, from 'Between the') Françoise Cachin and Charles S. Moffett in collaboration with Michel Melot, *Manet, 1832–1883*, © Editions de la Réunion des Musées Nationaux, Paris 1983; © 1983 by The Metropolitan Museum of Art, New York, *Manet, 1832–1883*, The Metropolitan Museum of Art; reprinted with permission. (pp. 131–2) Théodore Duret, *Manet*, translated by J. E. Crawford Flitch, Crown Publishers, New York, 1937. (pp. 130–1: Proust, first two paragraphs; 142: Jenniot; 154–5: Mallarmé) Robert Gordon and Andrew Forge, *The Last Flowers of Manet*, translations by Richard Howard, Harry N. Abrams, Inc, 1986. (pp. 133: Morisot; 140–2: Manet's preface; 145: Gautier; 145: Saint-Victor; 145–6: Zola, except last paragraph; 148–9: Fervacques, to 'famous Mürr' only; 152: Baudelaire to Thoré; 153: Baudelaire to Mme Meurice; 154: Zola) George Heard Hamilton, *Manet and his Critics*, Yale University Press, 1954; copyright 1954 by Yale University Press; used by permission of the publisher. (p. 133) George Moore, *Confessions of a Young Man*, edited by Susan Dick, McGill-Queen's University Press, 1972 (originally published in 1888). (pp. 155–8) John Rewald, *The History of Impressionism*, 4th revised edition, The Museum of Modern Art, New York; used with permissions of the publisher and Sabine Rewald, executor of the Estate of John Rewald.

Françoise Cachin,
formerly the director of the Musée d'Orsay in Paris,
now heads the Musées Nationaux in France.
She has organized many exhibitions,
including one on Italian Futurism (1973),
'Manet' (1983), 'Gauguin' (1988), 'Seurat' (1991)
and on the painters' Europe (1993).
She has written numerous catalogues and
works on Gauguin, Signac, Manet
and the monotypes of Degas and is the author of
Gauguin: The Quest for Paradise
in the New Horizons series.

For Charlotte

© Gallimard/Réunion des Musées Nationaux 1994

English translation © Thames and Hudson Ltd,
London, 1995

Translated by Rachel Kaplan

British Library Cataloguing-in-Publication Data

A catalogue record for this book is available from
the British Library

ISBN 0–500–30050–X

Printed and bound in Italy
by Editoriale Libraria, Trieste